Masters el Study
in Education

Masters Level Study in Education

A Guide to Success for PGCE Students

Neil Denby, Robert Butroyd, Helen Swift,
Jayne Price and Jonathan Glazzard

Open University Press

Open University Press
McGraw-Hill Education
McGraw-Hill House
Shoppenhangers Road
Maidenhead
Berkshire
England
SL6 2QL

email: enquiries@openup.co.uk
world wide web: www.openup.co.uk

and Two Penn Plaza, New York, NY 10121—2289, USA

First published 2008

A catalogue record of this book is available from the British Library

ISBN-13: 978-0-33-5234141 (pb) 978-0-33-5234134 (hb)
ISBN-10: 0-33-523414-3 (pb) 0-33-523413-5 (hb)

Typeset by Kerrypress, Luton, Bedfordshire
Printed and bound in the UK by Bell and Bain Ltd, Glasgow

Fictitious names of companies, products, people, characters and/or data
that may be used herein (in case studies or in examples) are not intended
to represent any real individual, company, product or event.

The **McGraw·Hill** Companies

Contents

Part I Study Skills at Masters Level

Part II Research Skills at Masters Level

Part III Written Outcomes at Masters Level

Part IV Case studies

Notes on the Authors

Neil Denby has been involved in teacher education for over 15 years. An experienced and successful author, he has written over two dozen texts at various levels from GCSE to post-graduate. He is a Senior Lecturer in Education and Partnership Co-ordinator for PGCE (Schools) in the School of Education and Professional Development (SEPD) at the University of Huddersfield. Research interests include using the abilities of gifted and talented students to enhance the learning experience and the training and certification of teachers in Citizenship at Masters Level.

Dr Helen Swift is the Head of Continuing Professional Development and Course Leader for the MA in Professional Development in the School of Education and Professional Development at the University of Huddersfield. Previously she taught in a variety of school and college settings. Her research interest is in the impact of continuing professional development (MA) on institutions, teachers and pupils.

Dr Robert Butroyd is a teacher educator of 16 years experience and leads the Business Education (with Citizenship) PGCE in the School of Education and Professional Development (SEPD) at the University of Huddersfield. Prior to this he taught Economics and Business Education in secondary schools for 14 years, including schools in the West Midlands, Yorkshire, and Galloway. His current research interests include teachers' occupational experiences and pupil disengagement.

Jonathan Glazzard is Course Leader for Primary and Early Years Education in the School of Education and Professional Development at the University of Huddersfield. He has worked in primary schools and has experience of teaching across the Foundation Stage, Key Stage 1 and Key Stage 2. He is actively involved in research in special and inclusive education.

Jayne Price taught for 15 years and was Head of Music and Continuing Professional Development Manager in an inner city secondary school in Leeds before becoming involved in teacher training in the School of Education and Professional Development at the University of Huddersfield in 2003. She is Subject Coordinator for the PGCE Music course.

Foreword

This book is written for post-graduate education students, who may be studying on a PGCE course or an MA, as well as those teachers who are taking Masters Level modules as part of a process of continuing professional development (CPD). This guide will be useful to teachers returning to study after a break to pursue an MA or to take a single module as part of CPD, or indeed those undertaking education studies for the first time. It will also serve as a helpful handbook for international students entering UK higher education for the first time. For such learners, this book provides an invaluable resource that will enable students to steer a path successfully through Masters (M) Level work.

One of the key strengths of the book is that it offers very useful guidance for teachers and those who are returning to higher education after a break from study. It guides learners through the MA process and gives them a basic framework with which to approach their studies. It reintroduces learners to academic conventions and the rigour of writing at M Level, and as such it will serve to bolster confidence and thus the likelihood of success. It provides a useful generic study aid for any students engaged in Masters Level work or PGCE study in education. Not all education students will enter Masters Level work from a cognate discipline and this text will introduce learners to the expectations, style of writing, forms of analysis, referencing systems, and so on that underpin M Level study in education.

The book has a number of significant strengths. It serves as a coherent guide to M Level study, taking learners step by step through the process. One of its distinctive features is the way in which it draws upon learners' assignments in the case studies to illustrate the expectations surrounding M Level work. It is one thing to describe the expectations surrounding this level of work, but what is so valuable about this book is that it ties these expectations to particular examples drawn from students' assignments. These assignments are quoted to illustrate particular points being made about M Level work. The case studies are presented at the back of the book. This will allow learners to contextualize the extract and will enable them to review the assignment as a totality.

The book provides a systematic engagement with the process of writing at Masters Level, showing the way in which literature can be used and evaluated. Importantly, it addresses the research process at M Level, offering guidance in conducting research and the writing of a dissertation. The book recognizes the range of assignments that can be used for M Level assessment and therefore not only discusses the traditional forms of writing such as the essay, the dissertation, the portfolio, but also considers other forms of assessment such as poster presentations, curriculum packages, and so forth.

Throughout this book the authors emphasize the importance of criticality. Although this is a contested term which can be bent to a number of different purposes, it is crucial for success at M Level study. It is also crucial for teachers to develop and hone such skills at a time when education is constantly subject to change.

The authors should be congratulated on producing an accessible and timely text that will surely contribute towards the success of M Level students.

Professor James Avis

January 2008

Preface

This book is designed to guide you through the process of studying, writing and achieving at Masters Level. You may be a post-graduate student in education on a PGCE course, a teacher in post, or a mentor in a school or college-based setting, helping trainee teachers to achieve. In whatever setting or position you find yourself, this book will aid you – or the person that you are supporting – in achieving Masters Level (M Level). Masters Level is a level of achievement beyond that of a first degree, implying not just deeper study of a specialized part of the subject area but, with this, a deeper understanding. There are key phrases that typify Masters level such as engaging with the subject or being critical and demonstrating expertise. The characteristics of the level of qualification are explored in the introductory chapter but, as you read through, you will quickly become familiar with them.

Focus

The primary focus of the book is on studying at M Level generally – on the knowledge, tools and skills that need to be developed for a successful outcome in an educational context. Our aim is to demystify the process by tackling those issues which in our experience students have found difficult. The book therefore contains a balance of practical guidance and exemplar material and takes a common-sense approach to studying and writing at this level.

Many post-graduate students (and teachers in post undertaking continuing professional development (CPD) at this level) have little idea of what is required to achieve at Masters Level, and no idea as to whether or not they can reach this level. There are conventions and guidance which need to be followed, and these are clearly explained. The book is designed to enable readers to do the following:

- Understand the nature of M Level work within education as a research-evidence-based profession.
- Understand how to prepare for such work by identifying a focus and a suitable process.

- Understand how to prepare, carry out and write a literature review.
- Understand the different methodologies and approaches that are inherent in M Level work.
- Understand the importance of ethical underpinning when working at this level.
- Develop confidence in making the transition from H to M Level.

The book covers the various elements of different Masters Level approaches to help both students and mentors in schools and colleges. The process of working at M level is not just about producing assignments, but about the thought processes, research and other skills that success at this level requires.

How to use this book

The book is divided into four Parts that naturally follow one another: study skills, research skills and writing up a research outcome are followed by Part IV containing the 'full' versions of the assignments (Case studies A–C). In their original state, each of these ran to tens of thousands of words so they have been carefully cut down to provide a 'snapshot' of crucial practice and to demonstrate expectations at Masters Level. Throughout, extracts from the case studies are used to illustrate specific points, to provide practice and to link with the exercises. To see the 'wider' picture, and to achieve context, the extracts can also be read in their proper place in Part IV.

Structure

Parts I–III follow in logical order the process through which Masters Level may be achieved. Part I details the expectations regarding good writing at M Level and explains basic writing skills such as paragraphs, cross-references and Harvard referencing. You may think that, as a graduate, these need little explanation. However, you may have graduated in a discipline that did not require writing of this depth, at this length, or requiring this degree of accuracy. Also, it may be a long time since you completed your degree and you may have forgotten some of the rules! The ideas of normal structure, elegant expression and lay-out conventions are explored along with guidance on plagiarism and referencing. We then identify sources of information and the breadth and depth of reading required at M Level including practical advice on how to carry out a literature review. The focus is on developing a critical approach and coherent arguments within identified themes. Key skills such as reflection and criticality are also explored. We then consider how to identify a focus and rationale for research, and how to embed this in both micro and macro contexts, paying particular attention to key drivers such as personal professional development needs, issues connected with pupils' experience and school and departmental priorities.

Part II investigates the major aspects of the research skills needed at M Level through an exploration of methodology, evaluation and developing criticality. Strategies for undertaking research and collecting data are outlined and, in addition, innovations such as listening to the pupils' voice are discussed. The focus then moves to the notion of learning from practice and developing evaluative skills. The concept of linking theory and practice is further explored here, to encourage you to synthesize the various parts of your M Level studies. Finally, the idea of criticality is developed and ways to demonstrate both your learning and your achievement are detailed.

Part III tackles the writing and presentation of assignments. It explains how to identify the main outcomes of research and present them in appropriate ways. It will help you to consider the impact of the research on your practice, your further professional development needs and possible avenues for further investigation. A specific focus in this Part is the building of a portfolio and the critical reflection that accompanies this. In addition, other, perhaps more imaginative, types of assignment at M Level are explored.

Case studies A, B and C are edited assignments and are presented to show you how to write the different forms of M Level work.

Chapter structure

Each chapter opens with an introductory paragraph that outlines the content that is to follow. On reading this, you can decide if this chapter is going to be of particular use to you at the stage you are at in your own studies. Chapters may be used separately, or combined with other chapters to give richer insights. Each chapter can stand on its own which means, inevitably, there is some overlap of concepts – it would not be possible, for example, to write a chapter on criticality and yet avoid mentioning it in sections on literature reviews, methodology or conclusions. Each chapter contains a number of pedagogical exercises and activities that can be carried out either on your own or with colleagues in group situations. These include brief tasks, many of which are open-ended and will promote discussion and disagreement (and so they should). Others are short exercises to help you understand a particular technique or level of response or to practise a particular skill. Many require you to use the extracts as primary source material.

Key Points are included at the end and in key places in each chapter. These consist of a brief list that summarizes the main points and can be used as reminders of the central tenets you will need to address. Each chapter includes an idea for an extended project or exercise to practise and underpin the skills discussed. Appropriate references are used in each chapter to promote further reading.

Exemplars

Each chapter is supported by appropriate reference to and extracts from three of the most popular methods of achieving at M Level: dissertation; curriculum package; and action research. The route by which you traditionally gained this level of qualification would have most probably been an extended essay or 'dissertation'. This is no longer the case as more imaginative and practical ways of demonstrating Masters Level skills are devised. You can see from our examples that, in addition to the dissertation, you could be asked to produce a curriculum package, a detailed study or a portfolio. Higher Education Institutions (HEIs) are aware that teachers (and student teachers) have busy and hectic schedules and now devise ways by which they can receive credit for work that they are undertaking as part of their usual duties. Thus, a student teacher may have to produce a curriculum package – the reflection on how it was delivered and how it might be improved could provide the M Level component. A teacher in post might have to put a new government ordinance into practice – an action research study of learning 'before' and 'after' could serve to show, on the basis of evidence, whether or not the innovation is effective. The final chapter looks in more detail at even more creative ways to achieve M Level outcomes. The methods chosen as examples are:

- traditional 'essay' or dissertation;
- curriculum package;
- action research study.

Chapter 8 provides details on the production and presentation of a portfolio assignment.

Appropriate extracts from each case study are clearly embedded in each chapter in the main text to support the learning outcomes at this level. The use of extracts in this way allows the reader to see the point illustrated and then continue reading, without having to search for the extract within the whole assignment. However, in order to also allow the reader to see extracts in context, and to see what a completed Masters Level piece might look like, we have included edited versions of the whole assignment (Case studies A–C). In each case, these have been edited not only to make them more manageable, but for ethical reasons, to prevent the identification of schools or individuals. Material that was not germane to discussions, evidence collection or outcomes has been omitted. Let's now discuss how each case study was planned and completed.

Case study A

Dissertation

This practitioner undertook the MA in two years because she had 60 credits through accreditation of prior learning (APLA). She works for a Local Authority as an ICT consultant working with teachers in schools to raise achievement in ICT.

Students are asked to critically reflect on an aspect of education in which they are interested. The projects usually relate to students' own professional roles and contexts. Students attend a dissertation day in October. The purpose of this day is to introduce students to the structure of the dissertation. Students are then allocated a dissertation supervisor. This can be any member of staff from the School of Education and, where possible, students are allocated to members of staff with appropriate expertise in the area about which they are writing.

It is expected that the experience will impact on teachers, schools and pupils. The dissertation is structured as follows.

Abstract

The abstract goes at the start of the study. It provides the reader with a synopsis of the research by summarizing the aims, the methods of data collection and the key findings.

Introduction

The student introduces the reader to the area for investigation and presents the rationale for the research. Students must justify why the topic is worthy of investigation and relate this to local and national contexts. The student clearly outlines the aims of the research.

Literature review

The student provides an overview of the key literature related to the area of investigation. Students are expected to cite a wide range of literature from books, journal articles, government publications, newspapers and web-based sources. Students must demonstrate that they have critically engaged with the literature.

Methodology

In this section students must justify their chosen research methods and discuss how ethical issues have been addressed. Additionally, students are required to explain how they have ensured that their research findings are valid and reliable. Students are also required to explain their sampling strategies, methods of data collection and analysis.

Analysis

In this section students analyse the key themes which have emerged from their data. Students present their key findings and analyse these in relation to literature.

Conclusion

In this section the students return to the original aims of their study. The students summarize their findings in relation to the aims of the study. Students are asked to make recommendations for the development of practice and consider how their research findings will be disseminated.

The word count ranges from 12,500–15,000 words for the whole study.

Case study B

Curriculum Package

This example of a curriculum package was written by a student following a one-year secondary PGCE course in Music. It was completed during the second school experience and was submitted in March, approximately two-thirds of the way through the course.

For this assignment, students were asked to create a curriculum package for a series of lessons for a particular group of pupils which developed their own practice in helping pupils to learn. The focus for the assignment and the class to which the package was taught were agreed with the university and school-based tutor. Ideas for the focus of the assignment included:

- teaching a particular topic area;
- the use of equipment or technology;
- the use of a particular strategy for teaching and learning.

The assignment brief outlined the various elements of the assignment that should be submitted:

Introduction (500–750 words)

This section outlines the context for the study, including brief details about the school and the class to which the package would be taught, the rationale for the focus of the package, including consideration of how the assignment would contribute to learning and professional development.

Literature review (1000–1250 words)

This includes an investigation of key texts from a range of sources related to the chosen focus of topic, teaching and learning strategy or use of technology or equipment.

Curriculum package (Equiv. 1500 words)

Students were to include the unit of work, lesson plans (lasting a minimum of 4 hours), details of use of ICT, assessment materials and resources for the curriculum package as well as lesson evaluations and observations of teaching.

Evaluation (1500–2000 words)

In this section, students were to reflect on the effectiveness of the curriculum package in terms of pupil learning and progress, interest and engagement. Students were asked to discuss both summative and formative assessment, outlining how assessment informed planning throughout the unit, illustrating the discussion with three examples of the work of pupils with differing abilities.

Conclusion (500–750 words)

In the concluding section, students were asked to evaluate what they had learned through teaching the package and make recommendations for the future, describing what they would do differently next time.

The assignment brief was developed as a trial in 2006–7 for implementation at Masters Level with the 2007–8 cohort of students. A number of revisions to the assignment brief in light of the trial were made:

- more guidance about how the curriculum package should be evaluated to ensure that this was more rigorous and more appropriate to an assessment at M Level;
- further guidance to encourage more synthesis between the theory outlined in the literature review and practice which is evidenced in the unit and lesson planning and the evaluation section of the assignment;
- further guidance given about narrowing the focus for the study, to enable more in-depth study with subject-specific suggestions and preliminary suggested reading given.

This example of the assignment has a strong focus but there are some weaknesses related to the other two areas of development.

Another major change is that the assignment is now to be submitted towards the end of the course primarily to enable the creation and delivery of the package to be much more informed by the reading and theoretical underpinning of the chosen focus of the assignment.

Case study C

Action research

This example of an action research project was completed by a student who is a practising teacher working in the Foundation Stage. It was the first assignment undertaken on the MA programme and was submitted in January.

In this assignment, students are asked to carry out some action research related to their own professional context. Students on the Early Childhood Studies route focus on a piece of action research related to teaching and learning in the early years. Typically, early years practitioners undertake action research within their own settings. Projects vary depending on practitioner's own professional contexts.

The assignment requires students to critically reflect on aspects of their own practice that they wish to develop or change. By engaging in action research, students are able to identify problems and issues in their own professional contexts and develop creative solutions to these. Some students have developed new approaches towards working with children and evaluated these as part of their assignment. Other students have developed strategies to improve the engagement of boys in literacy. Projects are exciting and innovative and students have the freedom to decide on the issues which are pertinent to their own professional context.

Students develop many skills through this assignment. They benefit through sharing their projects with fellow students and they become more critical of their own practice. Busy practitioners rarely have the time to reflect critically on their own practice. However, this project enables the students to stand back, think about the issues which need to be addressed and find solutions to these problems. The students evaluate the impact of their action research through a range of research methods.

The project enables students to share solutions to the issues which practitioners must address in early years settings. It encourages the students to be reflective about their own practice and to see teaching as a research-based profession.

Acknowledgements

The authors would like to record their grateful thanks to the three Masters Level students who have so kindly allowed their work to be used as exemplars in this book.

List of abbreviations

Education is an area which seems to coin new acronyms with alarming regularity. It is almost as if an idea or organization has no validity unless it can be shortened to a collection of letters. Never let an acronym pass without making sure that you understand what it means!

AfL	Assessment for Learning
APLA	accreditation of prior learning
AST	advanced skills teacher
BERA	British Educational Research Association
CAT	cognitive ability test
CPD	continuing professional development
CUREE	Centre for the Use of Research and Evidence in Education
DCSF	Department for Children, Schools and Families
DfES	Department for Education and Skills (now DCSF)
EAL	English as an additional language
ECM	Every Child Matters
FE	Further Education
GNVQ	General National Vocational Qualification
GTCE	General Teaching Council for England
GTP	Graduate Teacher Programme
HEI	Higher Education Institution
HMI	Her Majesty's Inspector
ICT	Information and Communication Technology
IEP	individual education plan
ILP	individual learning plan
LA	Local Authority
LftM	leading from the middle
LSA	learning support assistant
LSC	Learning and Skills Council
MFL	modern foreign languages
NFER	National Foundation for Educational Research
NPQH	National Professional Qualification for Headship
NQT	newly qualified teacher
NVQ	National Vocational Qualification
Ofsted	Office for Standards in Education

PGCE	Post Graduate Certificate in Education
PPD	postgraduate professional development
QCA	Qualifications and Curriculum Authority
QTS	qualified teacher status
SATS	standard assessment tests
SEF	self-evaluation form
SEN	special educational needs
SLT	Senior Leadership Team
SMART	Specific, Measurable, Achievable, Realistic and Time-related
SMT	Senior Management Team
TDA	Training and Development Agency for Schools
UCET	Universities Council for the Education of Teachers
VLE	Virtual Learning Environment

Introduction

Why would you wish to achieve at a higher level than Honours?

University degrees, at the end of three years study, are usually awarded at Honours level. The best receive the coveted 'First' – a First Class Honours. For many others an Upper Second or 2.1 is sufficient. What used to be called (in less enlightened times) the 'gentleman's degree' was the 2.2. or Lower Second – indicating that the candidate had done enough, but probably also enjoyed the social side of university life. Enjoying it too much, to the detriment of your studies, led to a Third. All work at this level is marked according to Honours level criteria and specific percentages are usually allocated to each degree level. Once this has been achieved, the next level is Masters. There is no 'easy step' from Honours to Masters Level work – although based on many of the same skills, it is really a different world.

In the field of education, there are a number of strong reasons that provide motivation for embarking on Masters Level studies. Most significantly, for those undertaking a post-graduate course of teacher training, is the Bologna Agreement. In addition, the profession of teaching, with government encouragement and support, has been recognized as a research-based profession. It has been accepted that improvements to teaching and learning are only possible based on considered research, properly funded. Schools that have already embraced this have seen its truth in the improvements to their own practice and outcomes. Third, education is an area where change is normal, and where teachers need to constantly update knowledge, skills and techniques. Think of the classroom where you undertook your own secondary education, then ask a parent or someone from a previous generation to describe their schooling. Imagine, then, what a teacher of 20 or 30 years ago would make of today's classrooms, replete with computers, interactive whiteboards and internet access, along with innovative seating arrangements and the novelty of pupils helping to make decisions! Yet, of course, teachers are still in practice after many years, but have changed their practice – they adapted, adopted, altered – to the benefit of their learners.

The Bologna Agreement

The Post Graduate Certificate in Education (PGCE) has, as a result of the Bologna Agreement, been subjected to a ruling stating that to remain as a post-graduate (rather than 'professional graduate') certificate, it must contain a significant amount of work at Masters ('M') level. The Bologna Process (1999) created an agreed equivalency of pathways for academic work throughout the European Union. The ruling took effect from the cohort which started in September 2007. The Universities Council for the Education of Teachers (UCET) carried out a survey in late 2006 to see if all Higher Education Institutions (HEIs) were planning to offer PGCEs at Masters Level. The result showed that 87 per cent intended to offer courses at M Level, either in conjunction with Honours Level (Professional Certificate) courses or on their own. Most institutions will offer 60 credits at Masters Level (a third of a full qualification) via either two 30 credit or three 20 credit modules. The majority of trainees will therefore have the opportunity to obtain a third of a Masters qualification and an excellent grounding for them to continue in their induction year and with subsequent professional development.

Continuing professional development (CPD)

Continuing professional development (CPD) has been recognized by the government as vital to the future of good education and funding has been allocated within 'the Children's Plan', the 'blueprint for the future' published by the Department for Children, Schools and Families (DCSF) in December 2007. It states that:

> We already have many teachers and headteachers who are among the best in the world. However, to deliver a teaching workforce and a new generation of headteachers which is consistently world class, we will allocate £44m over the next three years to make teaching a Masters-level profession, with all new teachers able to study for a Masters-level qualification through a focus on continued professional development.

The Training and Development Agency (TDA) offers HEIs funding for postgraduate professional development (PPD) for educational practitioners who have qualified teacher status (QTS). PPD is available through Masters Level courses. The TDA website states:

Course providers can tailor their programmes so that the content is negotiated by the school and its staff, allowing teachers to focus their learning in their particular school context – often through action research centred on the workplace. These pieces of independent study are often related to whole school improvement and can be integrated into school development plans and self-evaluation processes.

Groups of teachers are also encouraged to work together.

Personal development and improved practice

You should develop the ability to reflect on your own writing and your own practice as well as that of others. The effective reflective practitioner recognizes that improvements can be made and is willing to make them. Static or stagnant teaching is characterized by those who see no fault in what they are doing and are happy never to question their practice. Mezirow (1991) explains the idea of reflection followed by re-assessment as a 'transformative' process. Your aim will be to reflect in order to transform some part of your professional practice.

To succeed at this level requires a three-pronged approach, which encompasses the skills associated with academic reading and writing and the application of these to your own practice.

Reading

Reading is about 'engaging with the literature'. It means not just reading the key articles, journals, chapters or books linked to your area of study, but demonstrating wider reading to put these into context. It means recognizing that just because John Smith says that such-and-such is so, it doesn't necessarily follow that this is the only valid opinion. Who was John Smith writing for?; when was he writing?; did he have an alternative agenda? (Even Shakespeare wrote to resonate with a particular political climate. His *Richard III* is written as sufficiently evil to please Queen Elizabeth I, while good King James VI and I is descended from heroic Banquo in *Macbeth*.) In addition, how sound are the arguments and conclusions of writers? Who contradicts them, and who concurs? Are the values and contexts within which they were written still valid? This is all 'criticality'. Unlike at undergraduate level where, to an extent, you are expected to defer to 'authority', at Masters Level you can allow your own voice to be heard – this is one of the key differences between the levels of work.

Writing

What do HEIs require from your writing at this level? Clarity, certainly; coherent argument; evidence of scholarship in research and methodology; and the triumvirate of 'higher level' skills of analysis, evaluation and synthesis. Analysis refers to the process of sifting and comparing evidence and opinion; evaluation is better thought of as making judgements and justifying decisions or positions; synthesis is drawing together the different parts of an argument so that each supports the other.

There are clear (and basic) rules. Write simply and with grammatical accuracy, following the rules of punctuation. Avoid complex constructions, don't coin phrases, use double-negatives or clichés and use the active voice wherever possible. Your tutors (and readers) should not have to try to pick the sense out of sentences such as 'It was then noted, however, that in the definitive period of action, whilst observation was taking place, the observee was not particularly distracted by the observer.'

George Orwell's advice remains apposite (and if you read nothing else on writing good prose, you should read his essay):

> Never use a metaphor, simile, or other figure of speech which you are used to seeing in print.
>
> Never use a long word where a short one will do.
>
> If it is possible to cut a word out, always cut it out.
>
> Never use the passive where you can use the active.
>
> Never use a foreign phrase, scientific word, or jargon if you can think of an everyday English equivalent.
>
> Break any of these rules sooner than say anything outright barbarous.

(Orwell 1946)

Exercise 0.1

Consider the following as a piece of 'academic' writing. What do you think is wrong with it? How would you improve it? A suggested answer is given on p. 7.

> It is essential for the efficacy of the research that the voice of the pupil is listened to. Their central contribution has been disseminated by numerous commentators such as Convery (1992),

Dadds (1998), Ruddock and Flutter (2000), Cooper and MacIntyre (1996), Nieto (1994), and Sammons (1995). Sammons opines that they make an essential contribution to overall pupil achievement levels while MacGilchrist (2005) agrees with this view, discussing younger pupils. Gray et al. (1999) expound that listening to pupils will make schools improve better and 'The views of pupils/students', according to Hannam (1998) are really essential to 'school improvement'.

Practice

This book is aimed at those who currently are, or intend to be, engaged in the practice of education, primarily those who are or who aspire to be teachers. Therefore, one of the key dimensions that you can bring to your work is that of your own practice, and considering how it might be improved. It involves thinking about how you achieve teaching and learning outcomes and how these may be accomplished more easily or efficiently. This is the 'reflective practitioner'. This practitioner recognizes that teaching is not static, but can be taken forward; that there are different ways to solve problems (and different problems to solve) and that one of the people best placed to observe and record practice and to attempt innovations is the classroom teacher.

Comparing outcomes

Obviously, expectations of quality at Masters Level are different from those at Honours level. The assignment outcomes and abilities to be demonstrated can be compared by looking at the bullet points below. You will notice that while Honours level outcomes do include critical understanding and analysis, there is a greater emphasis on knowledge and understanding.

Honours Level assignment outcomes

- Demonstrates knowledge and understanding of teaching and learning strategies.
- Demonstrates knowledge and understanding of requirements and arrangements for the subject/curriculum area in the age ranges they are trained to teach.

- Critically understands the subject/curriculum area and related pedagogy.
- Shows a knowledge and understanding of relevant statutory and non-statutory guidance and policies for a subject/curricular area.
- Synthesizes theory and practice.
- Critically analyses and reflects on pedagogy.
- Critically assesses teaching and learning within the subject specialism.

Masters Level assignment outcomes

- Demonstrates addressing the title, the aims of the assignment and learning outcomes.
- Demonstrates a range of depth in the use of literature and materials.
- Uses critical analysis: breakdown and examination of issues and the inherent relationships between parts.
- Demonstrates the application of conceptual ideas and theory to professional practice.
- Provides an evaluation of theory and research in the context of professional practice.
- Provides enunciation, development and support of a case or argument.
- Demonstrates organization and control over complex material.
- Presents ideas, information and material in a clear and coherent manner using the Harvard referencing system.

Exercise 0.2

Consider the M Level criteria above. How do you think each of these could be demonstrated in a very good submission? Answer on p. 8.

Terminology

In this book, the authors talk of notions such as 'criticality' and 'the reflective practitioner'. They refer to 'reviewing literature' and 'generalizability'; to 'scaffolding', 'synthesizing' and to writing 'with authority'. They mention 'validity', 'reliability', 'triangulation' and 'ethics'. All these are key features of work at this level, but what do they mean? Each term or idea is described in detail in its proper place short definitions that follow should mean that you are not thrown by a term if you encounter it elsewhere.

The whole crux of Masters Level work is that you show a degree of 'mastery' of the area under investigation. This is demonstrated by showing that you know what has been written about the area (a literature review), can discuss its features and failings and recognize the points of consent and contention (criticality). You can then look at your own practice (reflection) and change it to improve an aspect of teaching or learning (reflective practitioner). To achieve this, you undertake research that harms or hampers no-one (ethics), that could be repeated with similar results (reliability), that is honest and open to discussion by colleagues (validity) and that may be applied more widely for greater effect (generalizability). Throughout this process you use frameworks provided by tutors (scaffolding), check outcomes carefully by cross-referencing with other research (triangulation), and bring various aspects of your work together to underpin conclusions (synthesis). Throughout you write clearly and with a knowledgeable voice (authority).

Key points

- You are embarking on Masters Level study because you want to, and because you can see a benefit to it. You are therefore motivated.
- There are several good reasons for M Level study in education.
- There is a step change from Honours to Masters Level work so you need to be aware of M Level quality indicators.

Answers to the exercises

0.1 The book does not always provide the answers, as many of the questions are open for discussion, but in this case, it is worth making an exception and pointing out the flaws in this passage.

It is essential {unsupported opinion} for the efficacy {not quite the right word: the thesaurus might give 'efficacy' as a substitute for 'effectiveness' but its normal usage is related to the effectiveness of specific interventions, such as medicine} of the research that the voice of the pupil is listened to {clumsy construction}. Their {singular pupil has become plural 'their'} essential contribution has been disseminated {spread, in the sense of 'sown' or 'scattered abroad' does not have the right 'ring' to it} by numerous commentators such as Convery (1992), Dadds (1998), Ruddock and Flutter (2000), Cooper and MacIntyre (1996), Nieto (1994), and Sammons (1995) {just a list, do something with it! Also, should be in date order}. Sammons opines {OK, acceptable, but it's a fairly antiquated usage, one of those verbs that has dropped out of fashion} that they make an essential {repetition} contribution to overall pupil achievement levels while MacGilchrist (2005) agrees with this view, discussing younger pupils {Lame, it needs more, why not quote the 'discussion'?}. Gray et al. (1999) expound {not quite right} that listening to pupils will make schools improve better {aargh!} and 'The views of pupils/students', according to Hannam (1998) are really essential to 'school improvement' {why split the quotation? Why use so little of it?}.

One way of rendering the same information more elegantly could be:

The importance of listening to the pupils' voice is central to this research. Key commentators include Convery (1992), Cooper and MacIntyre (1996), Dadds (1998) and Ruddock and Flutter (2000). Nieto (1994) discusses its importance, while Sammons (1995) points to increases in overall pupil achievement from listening to (and acting on) pupil opinions. Day (1992) considers that one of the ways in which teachers can act as role models for students is by listening to them. MacGilchrist et al. (2005: 65) believe that pupils have much to teach us:

> Particularly, we learn how articulate and in touch even the youngest pupils can be when they are given time to talk about their learning and their experience of it at school.

Gray et al. (1999) agree that schools which combine paying heed to pupils' views with any of the suggested approaches to school improvement will achieve a more speedy improvement while Hannam (1998: 3) is of the opinion that: 'The views of pupils/students represent the single most neglected source of potential data for school improvement.'

0.2 A 'very good' pass will have the following characteristics:

- The assignment title and aims are thoroughly addressed in a detailed and well-balanced fashion.
- Knowledge of subject matter is free from errors and confusions and is applied to professional practice with confidence and insight.

- Issues are critically analysed through skilled synthesis of relevant literature and professional experience.
- The line of argument is well developed, evaluative and consistently supported by reference sources.
- The writer has identified the implications and relevance of present knowledge and experience to future practice.
- There is evidence of flair and originality of thought throughout.

References

Convery, A. (1992) Insight, direction and support: a case study of collaborative enquiry in classroom research, in C. Biott and J. Nios (eds) *Working and Learning Together for Change*. Maidenhead: Open University Press.

Cooper, P. and MacIntyre, D. (1996) The importance of power-sharing in classroom learning, in M. Hughes (ed.) *Teaching and Learning in Changing Times*. Oxford: Blackwell.

Dadds, M. (1998) Supporting practitioner research: a challenge, *Educational Action Research*, 6: 39–52.

Gray, J., Hopkins, D., Reynolds, D., Wilcox, B., Farrell, S. and Jesson, D. (1999) *Improving Schools: Performance and Potential*. Buckingham: Open University Press.

Hannam, A. (1998) cited in J. Ruddock and J. Flutter (2000) Pupil participation and pupil perspective: 'Carving a new order of experience', *Cambridge Journal of Education*, 30(1): 75–89.

MacGilchrist, B., Myers, K. and Reed, J. (2005) *The Intelligent School*, 2nd edn. London: Sage.

Mezirow, J. (1991) Transformation dimensions of adult learning, in M. Welton (ed.) *Defense of the Lifeworld Critical Perspective on Adult Learning*. New York: SUNY Press.

Nieto, S. (1994) cited in J. Ruddock and J. Flutter (2000) Pupil participation and pupil perspective: 'Carving a new order of experience', *Cambridge Journal of Education*, 30(1): 75–89.

Orwell, G. (1946) Politics and the English language, *Horizon*.

Ruddock, J. and Flutter, J. (2000) Pupil participation and pupil perspective: 'Carving a new order of experience', *Cambridge Journal of Education*, 30(1): 75–89.

Sammons, P.M. (1995) Gender, ethnic and socio-economic differences in attainment and progress: a longitudinal analysis of student achievement over nine years, *British Educational Research Journal*, 21(4): 465–85.

The Children's Plan. Available at www.dfes.gov.uk/publications/childrensplan.

Part I
Study Skills at Masters Level

1 Writing at M Level
Good practice in essay writing

People think that I can teach them style. What stuff it all is! Have something to say, and say it as clearly as you can. That is the only secret of style.

(Matthew Arnold, 1822–1888)

Introduction

This chapter presents an introduction to the conventions and expectations of academic writing at Masters Level. Good writing is inextricably linked to wide reading. You will learn a great deal about academic style through reading journal articles and other texts. However, some caution is needed as some journal articles are often written in ways that make the content inaccessible to the reader. Clarity of expression is essential. Some authors try very hard to be too 'academic'. The result is that their writing is incomprehensible and sounds pompous and this should be avoided. As writers, we should aim for our readers to understand what we are writing about. Some articles in journals have to be read and re-read several times before they become even slightly comprehensible. This largely renders them useless, especially if the aim of the article is to impact on practice or advance social justice. Writing should be clear, concise, and complex terminology should be explained to the reader.

That said, it is important to remember that you are writing for an academic audience. Therefore, there are certain assumptions that you can make. For example, you do not need to spell out to readers that Key Stage 1 focuses on the education of pupils aged 5–7. They already know that! This is one example of unnecessary description. Generally, you should avoid description in your academic writing. For example, rather than describing a particular theory of learning, it is better to explore the criticisms of it. In other words, it is necessary to move from the descriptive level to the *reflective level*.

The focus of your writing should therefore be on exploring the issues related to the topic about which you are writing. Successful M Level writers focus on the issues and problems associated with the field of enquiry rather than describing it. The aim of academic writing at this level is to problematize, i.e. to explore the problems, issues and criticisms associated with the topic. Successful writers draw on a wide range of literature to do this effectively.

An essay on the history of Special Educational Needs would be very descriptive if it presented the reader with a description of the significant legislation of the past 30 years. To move this to the reflective level, the writer needs to explore the problems and issues associated with the legislation and the criticisms of the various Acts of Parliament. A study of the teaching of reading would be descriptive if it presented the reader with an overview of the stages through which children progress when they learn to read. A more reflective account would explore the criticisms of theoretical frameworks, which have been proposed as models of reading development. Successful students at M Level continuously question commonly held assumptions. They also explore the criticisms of theories, models, frameworks, legislation and new agendas.

Tutors need to feel the criticality within a piece of M Level writing. Successful writing will also challenge the reader's own thinking. The writer should explore the viewpoints in the literature and question them, dispute them or validate them. Theoretical frameworks and theories of learning should be questioned and criticized. Government publications and educational initiatives and agendas should be subjected to the same level of critical scrutiny. In short, successful writers take nothing for granted.

Tutor support

You will be offered tutorial support to enable you to complete your piece of work successfully. You will be offered both formative and summative assessment opportunities. The formative assessment is generally used to allow you to demonstrate planning, provide indicative references and show that you are 'on the right track'. Don't make the mistake of treating the summative assessment as an end in itself – it can be used as formative assessment towards a subsequent assignment.

Neither you nor your tutor want the work to fail. No one stands to gain through this. However, work that is not well written and is poorly expressed cannot pass. Work that lacks critical discussion and is largely descriptive also cannot pass. Therefore, it is important that you make the best use of your tutorial time. A substantial part of tutorial discussions should focus on how you can develop a critical and reflective discussion. Your tutor will help you to question commonly held assumptions and will help you to engage in a critical manner with the field of enquiry. A knowledgeable tutor will introduce you to texts that will help you to generate a critical debate. It is vital that you make use of this tutorial support. Your tutor will have a great deal of experience in marking work at this level and in educational theory in general. However, the onus is on you to maintain contact with your tutor and to ensure that the focus of the tutorials is related to what you need. You need to be proactive and ensure that you ask the right questions in tutorial sessions that will help you to engage with the topic in a critical and thoughtful manner. Therefore it is essential that you do some reading prior to these sessions. Nothing is more irritating to a busy tutor than a student who comes to a tutorial unprepared and with a limited number of ideas. Your tutor will be more than happy to help you if you can also demonstrate that you have put in the same level of commitment.

Further advice on reading is given in Chapter 2 and on developing a critical voice in Chapter 6. The rest of this chapter will look at the technical issues associated with academic writing at M Level.

Key points

- Avoid excessive description in your work.
- Be critical – challenge viewpoints and question assumptions.
- Explore the issues associated with your field of enquiry.

Expression

It goes without saying that accurate expression is essential at this level. On a simplistic level, this means ensuring that your work is error-free. Tutors find it offensive to mark work with careless spelling and punctuation errors. This is clearly unacceptable. To avoid this, a critical friend should proofread your work carefully. Someone else reading your work will often spot mistakes that you have missed. It is not your tutor's responsibility to detect these types of errors, either at the draft stage or at the stage of final submission. Tutors cannot and should not be expected to engage in microscopic marking. Work presented to tutors should therefore be error-free.

It is essential that you organize your work into logical paragraphs. A paragraph contains a number of points that are linked in some way. Tutors find it annoying when students present them with two-line paragraphs. Try to develop your paragraphs fully and at the end of each paragraph try to write a sentence that makes a link to the next paragraph. You will also need to develop an academic style of writing. To help to achieve this it is recommended that you write in the third person.

Exercise 1.1

Smith (2003) identifies over thirty variables that have been linked to underachievement such as socio-economic group and free school meal entitlement. Sammons et al. (1994) identified six groups of variables which linked socio-economic status and attainment including; pupils' personal characteristics, family structure, socio-economic factors; parent education, ethnicity and other. Baker (1998) believes that the main area for concern in underachievement is from low-income families. Kutnick (2000) argues that factors such as home background and school structures are influential. Tymms (2003) contend that the size of the school is an important factor.

(Case study A)

Explain how the writer uses a variety of language to introduce viewpoints from the literature. Suggest other ways in which this could have been achieved.

Structure

You need to plan your work carefully into various sections. Your assignment details may provide you with a writing frame, which will help you to structure your work. If you are not provided with a writing frame you will have to structure your own work into appropropriate sections. For the purposes of this chapter it will be assumed that you are carrying out a traditional piece of empirical research, in which case the structure adopted could be as follows:

- Abstract
- Introduction

- Literature review
- Methodology
- Analysis
- Conclusion.

Abstract

This will be a short statement (approximately 150–200 words) where you outline the aims and purposes of your research study, your chosen research methods, including samples and your key findings.

Introduction

In the Introduction you should provide contextual information about the research institution. For example, you could include the size of the institution, data on attainment and achievement of learners and factors that influence this, such as the socio-economic context.

You then need to provide a rationale for your research. It is here where you tell the reader why you are researching your chosen topic. In essence, you are justifying the worth of your study. The rationale can be examined on two levels:

1 *The local context:* Tell the reader what the issues are within the research institution, for example, has there been a fall in standards in a particular subject? Have informal observations and conversations with colleagues led you to believe there is a problem with an aspect of learning? Have Ofsted reports identified issues within the institution? Has school performance data indicated that there is a problem with a particular area of learning? Try to support your rationale with evidence (such as school results tables, inspection reports and information from improvement plans).

2 *The national context:* This is where you draw on the literature to determine whether there is a national problem with the local issue you have described. For example, you may have identified in the local context that boys are underachieving in your school. This is also a national issue and is supported by a wide literature base. Therefore, introducing the reader to wider literature on the issue will strengthen the rationale for your research.

You then need to identify the aims of your research. These need to be expressed clearly and succinctly. Avoid the temptation to include too many aims. It is better to keep your study focused.

Literature review

Start with an opening paragraph outlining the content to be covered in this section. In this section you will present the reader with an outline of the key literature related to your field of study. You need to discuss with your supervisor which key texts and writers you might cite in this section. However, you cannot include everything you read and you will need to define the parameters of your literature review. It is best if you can identify the key themes you intend to read about in the literature at the start, prior to doing any reading. (Further details on this, and other aspects of reading, are given in Chapter 2.) This will then give you a focus for your research. You need to identify the theories or theoretical frameworks you will include in this section. Clarify the theoretical content of your literature review through discussions with your tutor. Eaglen (Case study C) identifies the relevant theories in her study about a child with autism, as illustrated below:

> Baron-Cohen (1995) suggests that people with autism have a lack of *'theory of mind'*, or 'mind-blindness' which means that they cannot recognize the mental states of others.

Once you have identified the relevant theories, you can then develop a critical discussion of the theories. You can explore the criticisms/limitations of the theories in the literature and you can apply the theories to a practical context. It is important that you are able to demonstrate an understanding of the inter-relationship between educational theory and practice.

Exercise 1.2

In the example above, how could the writer have made links between theory of mind and practice?

Organise your literature review into sub-sections using sub-headings. You need to aim to produce a critical review of the literature. A good way to proceed is to model your literature review on a funnel. Start by citing the broader literature on the topic, then narrow the focus by concentrating on one or two key articles, which you can use as a basis for a critical discussion. (Further advice on how to produce a critical discussion is provided in Chapter 6.) The literature review should end with a summary of the key research findings.

Methodology

Start with an opening paragraph outlining the content to be covered in this section. In the methodology section you need to justify your research methods to the reader. However, you also need to acknowledge the limitations of these methods. You need to discuss ethical issues associated with your research and how you have addressed these. You need to discuss the specific procedures you adopted, such as your sampling strategy, sample sizes, methods of data collection and data analysis. You also need to show the reader how you have made your research valid and reliable. Acknowledge the limitations of your study in this section. Organize this section into appropriate sub-sections using sub-headings and draw on the literature written about methodology throughout this section. The methodology section should end with a summary of the research methods to be adopted and the samples used in the research. (Further detailed advice on methodology is provided in Chapter 4.)

Analysis

Start with an opening paragraph outlining the content to be covered in this section. Try to organize your research findings into themes. These can be explored as sub-headings. Therefore prior to writing this chapter it is necessary to identify the themes which have emerged from your data. Decide, on the data you are going to present. You cannot present it all! Data can be presented in the form of quotations from interviewees, field notes in the case of observational work and graphs, charts and tables for numerical data. Then you need to discuss your findings. Discuss the implications of your findings for a range of stakeholders *and relate your findings to literature*. You need to summarize the key findings at the end of this section.

Conclusion

Summarize your key findings in relation to the original aims of your study, as outlined in the Introduction. Then discuss how you intend to disseminate your findings in order to impact on practice, particularly for the research institution. Then discuss if any further research is needed and what form this might take.

Key points

- Your work should make use of sub-headings throughout. These act as signposts for the reader.
- Draw on literature throughout your study, not just in the literature review.

different from seeing a school primarily as a learning community. A learning community exists for a certain purpose – to promote learning – and will attend to and value its clients as learners, not just as people in general. The hard, inescapable fact is that learning, however broadly defined, is a particular kind of human activity ...which different people may be more or less good at.

Short quotations

Short quotations do not need to be indented and can fit smoothly within the text. Single quotation marks should be used and a reference for the quotation should be provided indicating the surname of the author, the date of the text from which the quote was taken and a page number. Again, it is not necessary to give the title of the text, as this will appear in the list of references. Some examples of short quotations from Case study A are listed below:

> Feinstein and Symons (1999: 306) contend that 'variables such as class size and teacher experience are usually found to have little effect on attainment'.

> Gorard and Smith (2004: 216) argue that 'the overwhelming majority of variance in school results is predicted by the nature (or prior attainment) of the intake'.

> Baker et al. (2003: 77) argue that 'there are troublesome conceptual issues involved in identifying membership of social classes'.

Exercise 1.5

Sometimes it is possible to put the reference after the quote. The following example provides an illustration:

> It has been argued that 'the interaction in focus groups emphasises empathy and commonality of experiences and fosters self-disclosure and self-validation' (Madriz 1998: 116).

Look at the following quote from Case study B:

> Kerry (1998) describes explaining as 'a complicated process' and insists that 'those who want to become good at it must analyse, practise and acquire the skills involved' (Kerry 1998: 120).

How could this be re-worded so that the reader is only introduced to the author after the quotation?

Secondary referencing

Secondary referencing is where you cite the research or viewpoint of an author but have not read the original text where that research or viewpoint was originally cited. Instead you have read about their work in another text. You should keep secondary references to a minimum. Where possible, you should consult the original text. This is because in secondary referencing you are only reading someone's interpretation of another's work. It is not always possible to access all the texts so some degree of secondary referencing will be inevitable, in which case you need to make it clear to the reader that you have not consulted the original text. Some examples of how to do this are shown below:

> Bullough (1998) writes about this when he argues that:
>
> > We cannot write just anything we wish ... interpretations, however tentative, must be disciplined by data, and ... we must proceed cautiously and carefully before proclaiming a plot.
>
> > (Bullough 1998, in Goodson and Sikes 2001: 56)
>
> Goodson and Sikes (2001) cite Plummer (1995) who has written about the way in which life stories can also be empowering to the reader.
>
> It is clear that the rationale for life history research is based on solid arguments. Goodson and Sikes (2001: 99) cite McLaughlin and Tierney (1993), who argues that narrative research allows individuals to 'name their silenced lives'.
>
> A perceptive comment is made by Hargreaves (1997) who is critical of the political demand for more quantitative data by arguing that it can 'promote a narrowly utilitarian and philistine approach to research and intellectual life' (cited in Hughes 2003: 11).

Using ibid.

In academic texts you will often see ibid. used when referencing paraphrases or quotes. Ibid. is short for ibidem, Latin for 'in the same place'. This is used when the writer is citing an author's work that has previously been cited elsewhere in the study. In the example, Bentley (Case study B) makes use of this convention: 'When teachers try to explain too much, they can often be met by the "enemy... the limited size of the student's short-term memory"

(Petty ibid.)'. Therefore, Bentley has previously cited this text and page number in the study immediately preceding this quotation, so there is no need to write out the full reference again. Ibid. is used only if the immediately preceding reference is the same as the ibid. reference. Writers may also use op. cit. (*opere citato* – from the work cited). However, you should note that the use of either of these conventions could be confusing. If at all in doubt, there is no need to use them – they tend to add nothing and may even detract from sense.

Completing the list of references

Follow the procedures for setting out a list of references laid down by your own institution. In particular, note carefully how to set out references for books, journal articles, web-based material, government publications and newspaper articles. References are set out in alphabetical order, using single line spacing, with a space between each reference. Different types of sources are generally listed together, so there is no need to list books together, then journal articles and so on. Tutors will check that all sources in the essay appear in the list of references and they will also check for a balanced list of sources such as books, journal articles and web-based sources.

Extended project

Find a critical friend to work with throughout the duration of your course. Ask your critical friend to proofread your academic work. Ask them to suggest ways of improving the work.

Key points

- Do not make unsupported claims or assertions. These must be supported with research and literature.
- Check your referencing guide and set out quotes and paraphrases according to its conventions.
- Avoid the over-use of secondary referencing.

2 Reading at M Level
Learning to use literature

The greatest part of a writer's time is spent in reading, in order to write: a man will turn over half a library to make one book.

(James Boswell, *Life of Samuel Johnson*, 1791)

Developing a literature review

This chapter identifies the reasons for writing a review of literature in your field of study and includes suggestions and ideas on how to carry out a literature review. Suitable sources of information for M Level literature searches are outlined, including questions to interrogate them. The nature of criticality within M Level is explored and ways for you to address this are suggested. The chapter also examines the breadth and depth of reading required at M Level using specific literature such as theoretical and research-based literature, government publications and policy documents. Key aspects of an effective literature review are specified.

The chapter clarifies the relationship of the literature review to an M Level assignment and concludes by presenting study skills which can be developed to enhance your literature review.

Why write a literature review?

The literature review is a critical examination of the existing theory and research that is important to your project. You will be expected to demonstrate quality in exercising judgement in assessing the coherence and relevance of literature, in relating this to practice and in evaluating the outcomes. You must establish a theoretical framework for the study through your literature review, thus setting it within the context of current often used interchangeably, for example: refereed, scholarly, peer reviewed or academic. These are the best sources to use in your study because the articles or papers submitted for publication are evaluated by a group of individuals who are experts in the subject area. Refereed materials assure the reader that the information conveyed is reliable. Depending on your theoretical framework, other journals may be valuable, even if they are not refereed, because they are professional publications which relate to your practice. An example of a refereed journal is *Educational Research* and an example of a professional journal is *School Leadership and Management* (both used in Case study A).

Key questions you need to ask yourself are:

- Is this a refereed or well-established professional journal?
- What are the purpose and aims of the writer?
- How has the writer developed his/her arguments to support the case being made?

Books

The main thing for you to remember about books is that they tend to be less up to date than journal articles, as it takes longer for a book to be published. The same points mentioned above about 'refereed sources' applies to books. They are a central source of literature and offer a good starting point from which to explore other sources of information. When tracing the history of a particular concept within education, books are a good way to establish the time frame.

As a guide to currency of information it is better to try to have a ten-year rule in terms of relevance (unless it is a seminal work which could date back over 50 years).

Questions you need to ask yourself are:

- Is the information up to date?
- Is the author a recognized expert in this field?
- Does the evidence being put forward support the assertions being made?

Theoretical-based literature

Theoretical literature is based on assumptions and beliefs that have been created within the social world. It is related to knowledge and deals with systems of inter-related concepts which may well be drawn from other writers' work. An example of a widely held theoretical belief is that of the 'reflective practitioner' which draws on the theories of Schön (1983) as outlined in the section on 'what is meant by critical reflection'. Denscombe (1998: 240) reminds us that in the social sciences we must treat 'theory' with more caution than we would if it related to the natural sciences. He argues that this is because of 'the complexity of social phenomena and because people react to knowledge about themselves in a way that chemicals and forces do not'.

Questions you need to ask yourself are:

- What is the methodology?
- What value judgements/belief systems underpin the theory?
- Is the author linked to an organization/institution/government body? Questions of bias or a particular way of looking at theory may be important.

Government and corporate reports

Many government departments and corporations commission or carry out research. Their published findings can provide a useful source of information, depending on your field of study. In the education sector such bodies as the Department for Children, Schools and Families (DCSF) (formerly the Department for Education and Science: DfES) and the Office for Standards in Education (Ofsted) publish many reports and documents. However, it must be remembered that these are not to be regarded as fact and should be scrutinized in the same way as any other information you have gathered.

Questions you need to ask yourself are:

- What is the status of the report?
- What is it trying to prove?
- Are there any other perspectives on this issue that do not come from government sources?

Web-based resources

There are many good education websites that give quick and easy access to information, for example, the government reports referred to above. However, if you are using the web for your research, you will need to develop the skills to evaluate the suitability of what you find. You will already be aware that some of the information on the web is unreliable and of dubious quality. However, it may be a useful starting point for your literature review. Wikipedia, for example, is not acceptable as an academic source but may be a useful starting point as it may indicate relevant academic texts or websites. 'Google academic' is a similar device for pointing you in the direction of good sources of literature.

Questions you need to ask yourself are:

- Have you evidence that the information is reliable?
- Is there an author and is s/he an expert in the field?
- Is it possible to follow up sources of literature which are referenced?

Key points

- As your reading develops your increasing knowledge, it will give you the basis to evaluate what has already been written in your field of study, demonstrate the relationships between different sources and show how this relates to your project.
- It is important to remember, however, that you are not writing just a summary of other people's work.
- You should analyse what others have written about the subject to underpin the originality of your own research, i.e. you have identified a 'gap' in the knowledge or have a new perspective because no-one has written about your context.

Critical engagement

M Level work requires critical engagement with the ideas of those in 'authority', such as authors of the above sources. Learning to be critical within academic enquiry requires a specific approach to your work, i.e. it has a particular meaning in academic study. Wallace and Poulson (2003: 6) outline what being critical in academic enquiry means and this includes:

- adopting an attitude of scepticism – not cynicism;
- a questioning approach to claims being made;
- scrutinizing – checking the coherence of a theory, checking sufficiency of evidence, checking for underpinning values and assumptions;
- keeping an open mind;
- being constructive.

They consider that becoming a critical learner requires taking responsibility for your own academic learning and having the motivation to inform your own and others' practice. If you present your own opinions, make it clear that these are your own and ensure that no unsubstantiated statements are made. Verbs such as 'could' and 'may' indicate that you are not making a claim of certainty but are suggesting a possibility.

When developing your literature review, you may find one or two sources of literature that you can relate to and the danger is to rely too heavily on them in presenting your review. To do so would mean that your arguments would not be balanced and you will be severely limited in your ability to provide a critical review. A poor engagement with literature would be where you presented chunks of material which were simply lifted from different sources and not linked together.

There is no doubt that you will have to deal with difficult concepts when engaging critically with literature. The dissertation (Case study A) provides a good example with reference to the term underachievement: 'there is no agreed or consistently applied definition for underachievement'. It explains that 'more recently academics are trying to define the term in order to clarify the meaning to enable it to be applied in a consistent manner'. The researcher has taken an earlier definition from the 1960s which she considers encompasses the widely held belief that underachieving pupils can be grouped by identified variables. Thus, she has acknowledged the difficulty of defining the concept and has made her position clear.

What is meant by critical reflection?

Working at M Level you are expected to engage critically with literature at a deeper level than on an undergraduate programme. There are various published models of critical reflection set out in the theories of Schön (1983), and exemplified by such writers as Kolb (1984) and Elliott (1993) that have been influential in professional education. Reflective practitioners develop their own 'theories in use' based on a range of factors, including their experience of similar situations, the knowledge of experts around them and their evaluation of the problems they are deciphering. Kolb (1984) demonstrates the importance of reflection through 'the learning cycle' which is outlined in Figure 2.1.

In this theory, learning is presented as a dynamic process that integrates direct experience, reflection on that experience, and the production of generalized explanations that can be tested out through practical application. The process develops from a two-dimensional cycle to a three-dimensional spiral as ideas are transformed through experience (Harrison 2003).

However, one criticism is that this tends to be a model of 'single loop learning', whereas at Masters Level you need to engage in 'double loop learning'. This involves reflection not only on what you do but also a

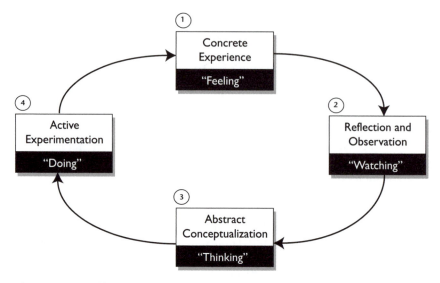

Figure 2.1 Kolb's 'learning cycle'

consideration of the reasons why; the assumptions that underlie your practice that may need to be revised (Argyris and Schön 1978, cited in Bennett 1997).

Key points

- It is best to avoid a 'source-by-source' treatment of literature. Instead, adopt a theme-by-theme approach that reflects your theoretical framework.
- The treatment of sources should be critical and analytical: key ideas and themes need to be debated and contrasted, not simply listed and described.
- Your reading will indicate that different writers will be making the same or similar points and these can be combined.
- The synthesis of material within the literature review, together with examples from writers who are making diverse claims, is a good example of critical engagement with theory.
- Through undertaking a masters programme you will begin to engage with critical reflection and double-loop learning which will be beneficial not only to your studies but also to your professional role.

Exercise 2.1

Read through the dissertation Case study literature review (Case study A) and pick out examples of where a synthesis of concepts and views has been achieved.

A range of literature and materials

The development of arguments which are theoretically underpinned is one of the key aspects of engaging critically with the literature. Different types of literature will tend to emphasize claims to different kinds of knowledge and have different sets of strengths and limitations which you will be expected to identify. These include: research, theoretical, policy and practice.

Research-based literature

This is based on focused and systematic enquiry and is a written account of research by someone in authority – i.e. someone who has a real insight into an issue – who has undertaken an investigative study using various methods of data collection and analysis resulting in a set of research findings. In this context, the word 'authority' does not mean a position of power but someone who has real insight into an issue. The quality of research is variable and often, to some extent, depends on who undertook the investigation and for what purpose. For example, a learned professor who has published widely and disseminated research through refereed journal articles and conferences is, perhaps, going to present a more acceptable account of his/her research than a novice action researcher. Although, you must remember, of course, that some widely respected research has been discredited at a later stage. Another point you should consider is the purpose of the research. Much of the research undertaken is funded and you must consider who the funding body is and how it could have influenced the research outcomes. The work may or may not be explicitly linked to a particular theory.

Theoretical-based literature

When discussing your own experience of your organization, you might wish to comment on different theories and their uses or deficiencies when applied to the real-life situation being explored. You should not use theory to merely support your ideas – again, remember to take a critical perspective and disagree as well as agree. Consider where other theorists have identified gaps or weaknesses or challenged the basic premises of a particular theoretical position. Theoretical-based literature will also be present in research-based works.

Policy literature

Literature derived from policy tends to emphasize knowledge from practice. It is based on a set of values and assumptions in keeping with a particular political ideology. In the case of an M Level project, you will find that it will often relate to policy which has been developed to impact on practice.

This is a good source of evidence, particularly because of its relationship to practice. For example, if you are an 'early years specialist' you would want to refer to the 'Every Child Matters' agenda (DfES 2004) and relevant legislation. This would certainly demonstrate that you are aware of what is happening in the educational field. However, there is a danger that you could get too reliant on this source of information, continually refer to it and give it the status of an indisputable document. All government policy should be open to discussion and debate; if you accept it uncritically, you are not demonstrating critical integration of literature.

Practice-based literature

Literature derived from practice is a very relevant source, particularly for the education researcher. A great deal of research/theory published in education is related to practice. What is being expected is that through the processes involved in developing your project, you will improve your professional practice.

Policy-based literature relates to knowledge of everyday activities of professional practice which could include teaching. This may be tacit know-how, i.e. going about your daily routine without having to think too much about it. An example of this for a teacher could be behaviour management. Reflection is the means whereby this tacit knowledge is brought into full consciousness in order to inform and challenge practice. In this instance it would require motivation to engage in critical reflection with the literature on behaviour management.

Key points

- The range of resources used is a key aspect of demonstrating the extent to which you have critically engaged with the literature and the materials.
- You can develop more credible arguments by not relying too heavily on one source of information.
- Choosing a variety of sources can also be a good way to validate your own ideas as well as providing different points of view.

Exercise 2.2

Look at the following examples of literature from Case study A and sort them into the above categories. However, as you progress with this exercise, you will find that categories are 'leaky' and in some instances the example could fit into two or more.

DfES (2006b) *Making Good Progress*. London: DfES.

Gorard, S. and Smith, E. (2004) What is 'underachievement' at school? *School Leadership and Management*, 24(2).

Hendricks, C. (2006) *Improving Schools through Action Research: A Comprehensive Guide for Educators*. Boston: Pearson Education.

Jones, S. and Myhill, D. (2004) Seeing things differently: teachers' construction of underachievement, *Gender and Education*, 16(4).

Learning and Skills Council (2006) *Key Learning and Skills Facts: Yorkshire and Humber, 2006–7* (online) available at: www.lsc.gov.uk.

A guide to a successful literature review

This section outlines aspects of an effective literature review. The examples given fit into either the 'effective' or 'ineffective' categories. The effective examples are from Case study A.

Exercise 2.3

Use your reading and experience to decide whether the examples are from reviews that were judged to be 'effective' or 'ineffective' and justify how you came to that conclusion.

Effective Review	Ineffective Review
Uses a range of sources of literature.	**Sticks to a few sources such as text books and internet.**
Example Dolton et al. (1999) argue that the National Curriculum and standardized tests have greatly increased the chances of pupils from poor background achieving the grade. ... Rashman et al.'s (2001) research indicated that at KS2 pupils on free school meals (FSM) results are lower than non-FSM pupils, with FSM being a direct measure of poorer families. Smith (2003: 581) categorically believes that 'pupils from relatively more economically disadvantaged homes were less successful as they were never expected to achieve the higher levels in line with their affluent counterparts'.	
Presents a balanced argument by taking into consideration the views of a selection of authors	**Relies on only one or two sources of information**
Example Feinstein and Symons (1999: 306) contend that 'variables such as class size and teacher experience are usually found to have little effect on attainment'. This, however, does not appear to reflect the view of Ofsted (1997: 9) that states that 'there are clear links between unsatisfactory teaching and low levels of attainment' and Wright et al. (1997: 63) who state that 'the most important factor affecting students' learning is the teacher'.	
Uses paraphrasing to connect the views of writers with similar vision.	**Only refers to the works of one or two authors and does not make connections between them.**

Example Jones and Myhill (2004: 531) claim that underachievement is 'concerned with potential not lack of ability' and that underachievement should be a measure of a pupil not doing as well as expected with the expected achievement derived from an IQ test. Both Jones and Myhill and Plewis (1991) explain this as being the view of the psychologists and accept that it is problematic as it relies on a reliable, independent measure of IQ.	
Keeps quotations short and pithy with linkage clearly made to its reason for inclusion in the literature review.	**Over-uses quotations and does not link them to the text.**
Example 'The ever-growing importance of scientific issues in our daily lives demands a populace who have sufficient knowledge and understanding to follow science and scientific debates' (Miller and Osborne 1998: 5). 'The current curriculum retains its past, mid-twentieth-century emphasis, presenting science as a body of knowledge which is value-free, objective and detached ... a succession of "facts" to be learnt, with insufficient indicated of any overarching coherence.'	
Adopts a thematic approach to the literature review.	**Writes chunks of material with little connection.**
The dissertation literature review in the Case study has followed an overall theme of underachievement, with sub-themes of community characteristics; ethnicity; the teacher's role; the role of adults in the home; prior attainment at Key Stage 2.	
Uses up-to-date sources of materials, unless quoting seminal works or following an historical time line.	**Uses sources which are over ten years old where material can be out of date and no longer relevant.**
Example It is widely acknowledged that parental involvement impacts on a child's attainment (Douglas 1964; Plowden 1967).	

Key points

- A good literature review demonstrates criticality, i.e. the ability to 'unpick' an issue or problem and to judge the extent to which relevant theories are clear and coherent.
- It should consider the extent to which the claims being made or the arguments put forward by a writer are convincing.

M Level assignments

When undertaking an M Level assignment it is important that you address the title, learning outcomes and aims outlined by the module specification. You should also make reference to the literature review in the analysis. These are an important guide to the development of the theoretical framework for the literature review.

Addressing the title

Addressing the title of the assignment may seem to be quite a simple task. However, many a promising piece of research has been let down by the researcher not addressing what the title infers. You should start by developing a 'working title' for the study as part of your planning framework as outlined above and then continually make reference to it and question if it accurately describes what you are undertaking. The title has direct relevance to the sources of literature with which you ought to engage. For example, if the title of a study is 'An Evaluation of the Effectiveness of Formative Assessment Strategies on the Quality of Writing at Years 5 and 6', then you could choose as one of your areas of literature 'Formative and Summative Assessment'.

Aims of the project

The aims of your project should be clearly articulated; three or four at the most are advised. You should constantly use these as a reference point for the project as they will form the framework for the literature review, methodology, analysis and conclusions. You should check that all parts of the literature review have relevance with regard to the aims to ensure that you have not gone off at a tangent in your discussions.

Exercise 2.4

One of the aims used within Case study A is 'to investigate the factors which have the potential to cause pupils to underperform in secondary schools'. Consider what you would choose as one of the key areas of investigation within the literature review.

Meeting learning outcomes

In order to achieve M Level work, you must demonstrate that you are meeting the learning outcomes of the module you are studying. These can be expressed in various ways but usually include the key words 'knowledge and understanding'. This gives you guidance on the knowledge you are expected to acquire and understand during the course of the assessment which is, of course, connected to the literature review.

An example of knowledge and understanding outcomes is given below for a dissertation module which relates to Case study A:

- Critically understands contextual theoretical and empirical research literature relevant to the focus of the dissertation.
- Critically understand the strengths and weaknesses of the chosen methodology and data collection methods.
- Has in-depth knowledge of appropriate data analysis techniques.

It is important that you are aware that knowledge is tentative and value-laden; there is a lack of agreement among experts about its exact meaning. It is also useful for you to remember that any review of the literature should reflect more than one kind of knowledge. Wallace and Poulson (2003: 23) refer to the use of different kinds of knowledge for different purposes. However, the knowledge itself has little value unless you can demonstrate that you critically understand the concepts and ideas that you are writing about.

Exercise 2.5

Read examples in the literature of different kinds of knowledge you could use in your project. List examples of these and consider how your value judgements could affect your objectivity in relation to these.

Analysis of findings

It is important that when you critically interrogate your findings you synthesize the main issues and underpin these with relevant literature, in particular, what has been examined in the literature review. If new literature to your study has appeared since you wrote the literature review, you can bring it in here.

Blend your discussion of theoretical principles and research findings into the analysis of your professional practice, and its organizational/national/local context, in order that direct comparisons and contrasts can be made and that issues, tensions and debates can be drawn out.

Exercise 2.6

Read through the 'Analysis and Discussion' section in the dissertation (Case study A) and pick out examples of where reference has been made to the literature review.

The literature review is not a stand-alone examination of the reading you have undertaken for the study. It is the basis for the theoretical framework of the project and is created from the aims of the study, module learning outcomes and should be related to the title of the assignment. In order to synthesize your assignment, reference to the literature review should be made within the analysis of findings.

Study skills for conducting a literature review

Using a thematic approach

It can be daunting setting out to write a 3000–4000 word literature review. It is unlikely that coverage will be exhaustive and consequently reading should be informed, selective and current. One suggestion is to choose three or four key themes which relate to the focus of the study and the research field. This will guide your literature search and reading. However, the areas must be interlinked and the reasons for choice of your theoretical framework (and hence your literature) should be clearly articulated in the introduction to the literature review.

Word count

It is very important to stick to any word counts given for M Level assignments. Part of the discipline in writing at M Level is being able to produce concise and relevant material. Often going over the allocated wordage could mean that you could have digressed in places. Many HEIs do allow 10 per cent flexibility either side of the wordage but do check this with your tutors. The development of a writing frame, as outlined below, is a good tool for imposing some self-discipline on the writing up of your project.

Writing frame

Taking the time to develop a writing frame before you commence your project is a good study skill to ensure that you keep within the parameters of your word count. This process involves you taking the overall total and estimating how many words to put into each section. It is understandable that certain sections, such as the Introduction and Conclusion will not carry the same weight as the literature review. Table 2.1 is a guide to how the wordage for a typical dissertation of 12,500–15,000 words could be apportioned. Having such a plan helps you keep within your allocated word count and put more weighting on the key areas of literature, methodology and analysis and less on the Introduction and Conclusion.

Table 2.1   A writing frame

Section	Approximate wordage
Introduction	2000 words
Literature review	3500 words
Research and methodology	2500 words
Analysis	3500 words
Conclusion	3500 words

Literary searches

You should get started with your reading as soon as you have formulated an idea for your project. The reading of one or two articles will provide the stimulus for you to seek out further literature and develop and refine your search. It can be very time-consuming so it is important that you make use of the excellent library resources available in HEIs. Libraries have a wide range of up-to-date source material, including electronic sources. Many journal articles/e-books are now available electronically through your library website and search engines provide easy accessibility. Make a list of key words from your initial ideas to use in your initial searches. It is useful to get into good study habits right from the start, so do keep notes of each article or text that you are reading. Remember to keep detailed accurate references (including page numbers) for all the materials used, and cite or quote from them using the Harvard system.

Texts and journals can also be accessed via a number of electronic search engines, some of which require a subscription. Examples include Metalib, BERA and the British Education Index (see websites below). It is essential that you record references as you read them, otherwise you may have a brilliantly apposite piece of writing, but be unable to later track down its provenance! If you are citing a web reference, you should also make a note of the date accessed.

Extended project

Look at the four titles below and suggest three sources of literature which could be related to each of the studies. Choose one of the projects and, using the three texts as your 'core' reading, list ten other pieces of literature. These should include a mixture of chapters from books, journal articles, extracts and websites. If you carry this out in a peer group, you can then compare lists with those of others and, in this way, see which literature may be considered central.

- A Study into the Cost and Impact of the Intensifying Support Programme and its Effect on School Improvement.
- Can the 'Big Writing' Initiative Improve Pupil Motivation and Help them 'Attain their Targets?'
- A Study into the Impact of the New GCSE Core Science Curriculum.
- An assignment title pertinent to your own studies.

Conclusion

Undertaking the literature review is the first stage on your journey of discovery. It may take many wrong turnings and send you down blind alleys but these all contribute to the richness of your critical reflection. Remember that writing a literature review is not an innate ability! It is a skill that can be learned. However, it requires motivation, an enquiring and open mind, patience and perseverance, and good time management. You must also develop the confidence to seek advice and guidance from tutors and to ask for clarification if needed when given feedback on your work.

References

Bennett, N. (1997) Analysing management for personal development: Theory and practice, in L. Kydd, M. Crawford, and C. Riches (eds) *Professional Development for Educational Management*. Buckingham: Open University Press, pp. 60–73.

Denscombe, M. (1998) *The Good Research Guide*. Buckingham: Open University Press.

Department for Education and Skills (2004) *Every Child Matters: Change for Children*. London: TSO.

Elliott, J. (ed.) (1993) *Reconstructing Teacher Education*. London: Falmer Press.

Harrison, R. (2003) Learning for professional development, in L. Kydd, L. Anderson and W. Newton (eds) *Leading People and Teams in Education*. London: The Open University, in association with Paul Chapman Publishing.

Hustedt, J. T. and Raver, T.C. (2002) *International Journal of Behavioral Development*, 26(2): 113–19.

Kolb, D. (1984) *Experiential Learning*. Englewood Cliffs, NJ: Prentice-Hall.

Schön, D.A. (1983) *The Reflective Practitioner*. London: Temple Smith.

Vygotsky, L.S. (1978) *Mind in Society*. Cambridge, MA: Harvard University Press.

Wallace, M. and Poulson, L. (2003) Critical reading for self-critical writing, in M. Wallace and L. Poulson (eds) *Learning to Read Critically in Educational Leadership and Management*. London: Sage Publications.

Wood, D., Bruner, J.S. and Ross, G. (1976) The role of tutoring in problem solving, *Journal of Child Psychology and Psychiatry*, 17: 89–100.

Websites

British Education Index http://www.leeds.ac.uk/bei/

British Educational Research Association http://www.bera.ac.uk/

Metalib http://exlibrisgroup.com/metalib.htm

3 Researching at M Level
Focus, context and rationale

Our knowledge can only be finite, while our ignorance must necessarily be infinite.

(Karl Popper, *Conjectures and Refutations*, 1963)

Introduction

Why do research? It can be time-consuming, demanding, and if embarked on for the wrong reasons and without a clear focus, stressful. On the other hand, of course, it can cement relationships with colleagues and learners, offer insight into professional experience, improve your impact as a teacher and can be enjoyable. It all depends on whether you can 'get it right': the right motives, the right focus, the right preparation. What is right for one activity, or group of researchers may be inappropriate for others. So, how does a budding researcher find out what is 'right' for them? In this chapter we offer advice for those working on a critical commentary for a portfolio-type assignment, a piece of action research for a module or for a dissertation.

This chapter is about understanding your own motives for researching a topic, finding an appropriate *focus* for that research, exploring the *context*, and explaining your reasons (*rationale*). This chapter is laid out under these headings. However, the process of developing a focus, determining the appropriate context and explaining your rationale is rarely a linear process. You will be constantly going backwards and forwards, reviewing each section, changing, editing in the light of what you are learning while you are doing your research.

Motivation

The first place to start is with your own motives for doing the research. It is important to be honest about your motives with informants, collaborators and other interested parties. Crucially, it is important to be honest with yourself. It may be that you are embarking upon research because it is a necessary part of the requirements for the Masters qualification you are pursuing. Maybe you had never thought of doing research, and it holds no great interest for you. If this is the case, then there is a tendency to feel guilty about this and pretend that you want to find something profound that is not only going to add to the world's knowledge but will also offer magic solutions for you and your colleagues. This is a mistake. You are, or wish to be, qualified in your field of work. This requires you to undertake tasks necessary for you to achieve or develop the status that your career offers. This is an instrumental reason for doing research. This involves your professional development and a contribution to the development of your institution whether it is a training organization, a school or a college. On the other hand, you may be excited at the prospect of doing research. You can see yourself working late into the evenings, travelling a road of discovery that nobody else has travelled, revealing truths and making connections that nobody else has thought of. You can't wait to get started. This is an intrinsic motive, and is mistakenly thought of as a more legitimate reason for undertaking research. It may be that you feel a bit of both. However you feel about doing research, you need to examine your motives and be truthful about them. This examination of motives has implications.

If your primary motive is instrumental, then those affected by your research need to know this, so that they understand that the person most likely to gain anything from the research is the researcher. Even if your motivation is weighted towards the intrinsic value, then the person most likely to gain from research, is still you, the researcher. Understanding this prevents you from making promises to people that you can't keep. Benefits to your informants that might accrue from your research cannot be guaranteed. It is wise not to raise expectations that may not be met. Research, write-up and dissemination take time. It is possible that a current cohort of your learners may benefit from your research (particularly if it is action research), but if there are benefits, it may well be a future cohort who would benefit more.

Choosing to start research is a big decision, for you, your colleagues, your learners, and possibly your family and your friends. Expectations need to be realistic. Your aim is to meet, or if you are really well prepared, and lucky, to exceed expectations.

A second implication is that it starts you questioning the assumptions we all take for granted. For example, in the course of carrying out the work of an educational practitioner, we learn certain behaviours; some are deliberately learnt, others we pick up by being around other practitioners. An example of this would be the practice observed in a secondary school whereby pupils always stood when a teacher entered the classroom – not the caretaker, not a technician – just teachers. When a senior teacher at the school was asked to explain the reasoning behind this, he couldn't. He said he had never thought about it, they had just always done it. As researchers we examine our reasons, actions and thoughts, and those of others.

The next section considers three areas that normally shape the first part or chapter (if it is a dissertation) of a written assignment at Masters Level. This next section is about the first, faltering, provisional step taken when doing research: choosing a focus.

Finding a focus

This first step should be re-visited throughout the research project until it becomes resilient to interrogation from others. Once a provisional focus is identified, the feedback from data collection and analysis may lead to further refinement of the focus and results in a robust and meaningful piece of research. This constant move from focus to data and back again is called *progressive focusing* (Altrichter et al. 1993). This often happens during the course of a research project; you start out thinking you are looking at one thing, then as you gather more information you realize that you are looking at an ever narrower aspect because you have discovered in doing the research that it is better to do it this way. Sometimes, in more extreme examples you may even decide that you have been looking at the wrong thing and are now looking at something else. The important thing is to be honest in what you write, and don't pretend that, as you decided the focus was (X) at the start that you will keep looking at (X), even though you have now discovered that it is better to look at (X-1), or the relationship of X and Y. For example, you may have thought that if you want to find out how you can help a group of 20 learners increase achievement that you should collect data from all 20. However, you find that significant data, data that raise issues, come from eight particular underachievers. You may decide that time spent with these informants would reveal more than the same amount of time spread thinly over all 20. A second example from the same group might be that you have found that there are significant issues regarding language support, so the relationships of that group with other informants such as language tutors, parents, etc. may lead to more significant findings. The result of this is that you have changed your focus from all 20 pupils, to eight pupils and their learning relationship with two language support teachers. The wider, and vaguer the area of investigation, the greater is the likelihood that the research will be criticized for lack of validity, i.e. it doesn't do what it says it does.

Practical considerations are important when deciding on which issues to focus. How much time, energy, money and support do you have? What resources do you have? The key to developing an appropriate focus is to turn issues into questions, and in the process to refine and limit the area under investigation so that the work that is then undertaken is achievable and meaningful. How do you decide what the focus is?

Here is a scenario. Consider it, and then draw up a list of what you think the issues are that could be the focus of any future research. At this point consider all possibilities. Inappropriate ones can be ruled out later. You should ask yourself what it is important to discover. Remember to question assumptions, including your own, and then compare your ideas with those that we have offered.

> A lecturer at Valley FE college is concerned about the motivation of her adult returners on an NVQ 2 in Environmental Conservation course. Many are indeed drawn to this subject because of their love of natural history. Although NVQs were principally designed to be delivered and assessed in the workplace, this NVQ is unusual in that it acknowledges the high levels of volunteer involvement in this area of work. 'Candidates', as students are called in NVQ terminology, can develop their skills and knowledge in a variety of ways and in a range of formal and informal settings: college-organized activities, including practical work with local partnership organizations; special projects with conservation organizations; regular volunteer activities; working holidays; paid employment. The nature of the NVQ qualification framework and the paperwork associated with it appear to be having a negative impact on learners. There is often a discrepancy between the high levels of enthusiasm for the subject area and student reactions to the terminology and format of the NVQ. The lecturer is worried about levels of achievement and retention on the course, despite the enthusiasm of these students for natural history.

If the text is read carefully there are a number of potential points of focus. One reading reveals the following issues that could be a focus of the work

1 How can the motivation of adult learners on an Environmental NVQ in an FE college be improved?
2 How can we reduce the negative impact of paperwork on the motivation of adult learners on an Environmental NVQ in an FE college?
3 How can the lecturer improve levels of achievement and retention on an Environmental NVQ in an FE college?

There could, of course, be other issues to focus on. These are offered as examples. Why do you think that the wording specifically mentions 'adult learners', and 'FE college' in points 1 and 2? How is point 3 different? Does it need to mention adult learners?

The priority given to the different points of focus is shaped by the professional and personal motives of the researcher, the micro (institutional) context and the macro (national/policy) context. All these factors will influence the focus and ultimately the rationale, or justification of the work that is to be undertaken. These factors are addressed in the second section of this chapter.

Research should have significance, and not simply be done out of curiosity for the trivial. One way of deciding whether a focus is worth pursuing is to try to describe the focus as a problem to be investigated. If an issue is not a problem for the purpose of your professional duties, then it may not be worth considering as a focus. For example, if there is low-level noise in a classroom, this may be distracting or irritating to you, but if it does not interfere with the learning, then it is not a problem for you in terms of your professional duty of teaching and encouraging learning. So, if you made the reduction in this noise level a focus for your research, it might be considered trivial. If you had evidence (perhaps from a research diary, or discussions with distracted pupils) that this level of noise was a problem for teaching and learning, then it might be a worthwhile focus of your research.

It is important to find out what others have written about your situation. You might find difficulty deciding what to read. Chapter 2 deals with this in detail. But, when starting out, a brief selection of literature on two or three topics that appear to be of relevance will start you on your way. You might look at a couple of chapters from academic books, or a couple of articles from academic journals. This will allow you to write a paragraph using these indicative references in your rationale. You can always return to it later.

Once you have determined what the problem might be, turn this into aims by asking what you hope to find out about this problem. At this point you might want to draw up a list of research questions. These aren't questions that you ask a key informant, they are questions the researcher needs to answer for themselves if they are to understand the research problem and possible implications or recommendations. Some people do this after the literature review, but it is perfectly acceptable to put them into your introductory section or chapter as it offers clarity to the reader right from the start.

Exercise 3.1

Read these aims taken from the dissertation (Case study A):

Aim 1. To investigate the factors which have the potential to cause pupils to underperform in secondary schools.

Aim 2. To identify the factors which could potentially be contributing to the underperformance of pupils in ICT at Key Stage 3 in the local authority.

Aim 3. To ascertain the factors which could have impacted upon the pupils KS3 ICT teacher assessment level in 2006.

Now read the dissertation and see if you agree with the focus the researcher has chosen as described in these aims. Do the research questions explore some of the assumptions or 'common sense' involved in the focus? Questioning 'common sense' is often a good thing to do. Understanding often isn't as common as you might think, and when you explore 'common sense' you find it often doesn't make much sense either! Would you ask any different questions, or leave any out?

Key points

- Select a focus that you can do something about. This will normally concern practice, or implementation – a practical task that is within your control. It is so much more difficult and stressful to look at something other people are doing.
- The focus should be non-trivial and should exclude as many variables as you can. This means that the focus should be as tight and limited as you can make it, while still being significant.
- In many ways, determining the focus can be the most difficult thing to do, and may delay your start. Don't let it.
- Make a start, and constantly revisit your focus, changing it as necessary as your research increases your understanding. This is called progressive focusing.

Exploring the context

In this section we explore the micro and macro context. Colleagues, students, pupils and other researchers may be interested in what you have found. If they want to learn from your work, among the things they need to know about is who carried out the research, where and when. The reader can then make an informed decision as to whether the research may have any relevance to them. The following headings will give you some ideas about how to shape the context section of your masters assignment.

The micro context

Formal and informal

How is the research institution organized, and how does it work? The way an institution is meant to work and how it works in practice can differ markedly. Practice may differ from policy. For example, if your research focuses on behaviour management, there may be a formal policy that requires instances of misbehaviour to be reported to a line manager. However, classroom practitioners may have a support system whereby they take each other's 'difficult' learners into each other's classrooms. This may be a stage that is not published in a policy document. If you were looking at systems of reward and punishment, it would be important to describe this informal stage of support.

Your position

Your relationship to colleagues, collaborators and informants will illustrate any power relationships or vested interests that may be relevant.

Your values

As a researcher it is difficult to put on one side the things that you think are important in education. Try as you might to be objective (and you should), it may well come through in your work. So, make your role in the situation you are studying clear so that a reader can identify any bias that is present in your work.

Collegial culture

Some institutions are 'balkanized' (Hargreaves 1994), where departments work in isolation from each other. Some colleagues work in isolation from their departments. Some institutions work in a collegial way, where co-operation is a flexible and optional activity. Some have co-operation thrust upon them.

It is important that we understand how educational practitioners, whatever their institution, relate to each other, as education takes place in a social situation. This means we all play a role and relate to each other in these roles. How we relate to each other will influence the experience of our learners. For example, do we share resources, learning experiences, good practice, or bad practice?

Subject/thematic aims

If you are researching within an academic subject there may be ways of seeing the world that affect what you find. Science may, for example, have a positivist view of enquiry (a search for 'knowledge' that is objective, that cannot be disproved), whereas English may have a humanist view, where interpretation of different experiences of 'knowledge' is held to be valid.

The influence of the learner experience

This is a significant factor in shaping the environment. How learners behave, learn, and are perceived are important influences on what the researcher considers to be important. What background do the learners come from, or live and work in? Have you considered issues of diversity, for example, social class, ethnicity, gender? What prior knowledge or experience do they have? How does the influence of the learner affect the practitioner (whether teacher, lecturer or trainer) and vice versa?

The macro context

Constraints

What legislative, accountability and guidance structures limit your work, and your research? Data protection legislation, National Curriculum, Ofsted, Every Child Matters, QCA guidance may affect you. What pressures are on you, or the research context from other stakeholders – parents, business, local community, the department you work in, the school or college you work in?

Constraints in themselves aren't 'bad' things. Constraints can also be opportunities. For example, funding may have been made available for new initiatives that may be creative, challenging, and exciting. They will also come with their aims and accountability structures.

Agency and structure

How much can you influence practice or research given some of the constraints we mentioned above? What freedom do you have to be a change agent, or an agent who can interpret these constraints? For example, can you emphasize one aspect of the curriculum more than another despite the constraints of Sats, Ofsted, league tables, or performance-related pay?

Exercise 3.2

Read this paragraph taken from the context of the dissertation (Case study A).

> Researcher's role
> Within the strategy the government recognized the need for high quality teachers to lead the strategies and support schools (DfES 2004a: 3). Therefore, when the strategy was launched, consultants were recruited from schools to work within local authorities. Consultants are match-funded by the national strategy and the LA in which they work. The researcher is in the privileged position of being the Secondary ICT Consultant ...
>
> This research is of particular interest as understanding what is preventing pupils achieving high standards and working with schools to improve teaching and learning will directly impact on the success of the consultant in achieving their objectives within the national strategy.

How might the writer's role influence their research? Will their position influence their attitude to 'teaching' and what it means? Might it influence their attitude to 'learning', and what it means? Is there any more contextual information that could usefully be included?

Key points

- Those interested in your work will have confidence in what you have written, and it will increase yours if you make it plain what challenges and opportunities you face.
- Micro and macro contexts are organizing concepts. They help you to analyse these challenges and opportunities.
- Don't forget the influence you have on the research. As a practitioner researcher you will try to be objective, but the concept of *reflexivity*, whereby the researcher inevitably impacts upon the research, suggests that this is not going to be entirely successful, so you must describe your role in the situation you are researching.

The rationale

What information should be included in your rationale? By this stage you should have a clearer idea of what you would like to focus on and why. In this part of your research you make clear what your thinking has been. The starting point is similar to the question which opened this chapter. Why do *this particular* research? You have a unique understanding of the focus and the micro and macro context. You should be able to write from a position of authority. The rationale builds on your early reading, progressive focusing and exploration of the micro and macro contexts. It explains your reasons for the focus of your research. It should be underpinned by reading to justify your choice of focus. The rationale should not be too long. It simply justifies why you are exploring a particular focus. It gives a flavour of what you are trying to do so that a reader understands at the outset that this is a serious study with a non-trivial focus.

Starting to write up your work is something some researchers put off until the latest possible date. You may have pages of rough notes, and plenty of data. You think the writing up will be the last thing you do. This would be a big mistake. Start writing your draft as soon as you can. Drafting and re-drafting is an important process. This approach can help you overcome what can be a psychological barrier. Begin by drawing up a list of questions a reader might want answered in your Introduction. Think about the issues we addressed in the focus and context sections.

You may well come up with better questions than we have. You may have extra questions that are not evident in those we have provided. You may consider some of our questions are not relevant to your research. Remember, you are responsible for your research and you should be in the best position to judge what is appropriate. Be open to advice, evaluations, feedback, opinions, and other perspectives. Your responsibility is to listen, critically engage, evaluate, and then adopt, adapt, or reject this advice.

The questions we have asked you to consider so far are designed to encourage critical thinking. This criticality is essential to Masters Level work. Being critical is not the same as being negative. Criticality involves recognizing that there are different perspectives on an issue, taking these different perspectives into account and developing a measured evaluation of the issue. Here are some issues you need to take into account when writing your rationale.

What brought the issues/problems you are focusing on to your attention?

It could be the dissonance created by what you read and the reality of your situation. It is useful if there is some documentary evidence of this issue. It could have arisen from a conversation with colleagues, or from data collected from your class or institution. It could be a theme that you have noticed

4 Methodology

> The best and most pleasant life is the life of the intellect since the intellect is in the fullest sense the man.

(Aristotle 384–322 BC)

Introduction

This chapter introduces you to the key aspects of the methodology chapter within a Masters Level piece of work. According to Clough and Nutbrown:

> A characteristic purpose of a methodology is to show not how such and such appeared to be the best method available for the given purposes of the study, but how and why *this way of doing it was unavoidable – was required by –* the context and purpose of this particular enquiry.

(2000: 17)

These writers stress that the purpose of a methodology chapter is to justify particular research decisions. It should *persuade* the reader that the methods chosen were fit for purpose, i.e. to answer the research questions identified in the aims of the study. This section should draw on the methodology literature to enable you to justify your chosen approach(es) and method(s). There should be a clear distinction between *methodology* (justification of approach(es) and method(s) and *methods* (specific procedures undertaken to complete the research).

The aim of this section is to be transparent and honest. You need to acknowledge the limitations and shortcomings of your chosen methods and approaches and to be honest about any problems/issues that arose along the way. Educational research rarely, if ever, runs smoothly. It is unlikely that things will run according to plan. Changes may need to be made throughout the process of the research. Time constraints (getting the work in on time) may mean that changes are necessary if the deadline is to be met. Students often realize that initial research proposals are too ambitious and the project may need to be slimmed down halfway through the process. Sample sizes may have been too large. Participants who initially agreed to take part in the research may withdraw for a variety of reasons in the middle of the research. These 'hitches' do not mean that the researcher has failed. The researcher must simply acknowledge the problems along the journey, make adaptations and continue with the research. Therefore, it is essential that the researcher documents the whole process in a research diary and this can later be added to the methods section of the methodology chapter.

However, let us first of all turn our attention to *methodology*. In this section, the researcher will aim to justify why a particular approach to research has been adopted. Approaches can be qualitative, quantitative or the researcher could adopt a mixed-method approach. Once the approach has been justified, the researcher can then present justification for choice of specific research methods.

Quantitative/qualitative approaches

Researchers often define themselves as qualitative researchers or quantitative researchers. Quantitative and qualitative approaches to research are often referred to as research *paradigms*. According to Grieg et al.:

> Qualitative research strives for depth of understanding in natural settings. Unlike the positivist quantitative tradition it does not focus on a world in which reality is fixed and measurable but one in which the experiences and perspectives of individuals are socially constructed.

(2007: 136)

Therefore, qualitative research places emphasis on the way in which individuals interpret their experiences (Holloway 1997). The data that are generated from qualitative research are often rich in description and detail. Silverman (2000) emphasizes that by definition qualitative research is stronger on descriptive accounts than quantitative research.

Quantitative research, in contrast, focuses on *quantities* and often involves the statistical analysis of large amounts of data. It is situated within a scientific model of research where hypotheses, controls and variables are common features of the research process. Therefore, quantitative research focuses on the measurement of causal relationships between variables (Denzin and Lincoln 2000).

Both qualitative and quantitative approaches have been criticized in the literature. Qualitative approaches are often seen as having less rigour than quantitative approaches and data are often viewed as being weak, inconclusive and anecdotal (Bryman 1988). The government also seem keen that educational researchers adopt research methods which demonstrate 'conclusively that if teachers change their practice from x to y there will be significant and enduring improvement in teaching and learning' (Hargreaves 1996: 5). This emphasis on cause and effect is situated within a quantitative approach to research. Tooley is critical of small-scale research, which does not produce generalizable data, as is often the case with small-scale studies:

> If research is to provide us with a serious contribution to fundamental theory or knowledge, then it is in general desirable to be able to generalise in some way beyond the actual sample used in the study.

> (Tooley 1998: 14)

However, Richardson (1996) stresses that qualitative research is a specialist field of enquiry with its own language and should not be classed as a soft option for researchers. Critics of quantitative approaches have explored the limitations of scientific approaches to research. It has been argued that the positivistic paradigm assumes that human behaviour is repetitive and predictable, resulting in a reductionist view (Hampden-Turner 1970). Habermas (1972) has also argued that positivism is unable to answer many important and interesting questions about life. In addition, Roszak (1970) emphasized the alienating effect of scientific research and the 'relentless pursuit of objectivity' (cited in Cohen et al. 2000: 18).

Essentially the research paradigm and methods to be adopted must be appropriate to answer the research question(s) which the researcher is trying to address. Silverman stresses that 'most research methods can be used in either qualitative or quantitative studies' (2000: 89), therefore it is too simplistic to locate research methods within a particular paradigm of research. As a university or similar student on Masters Level programme you must justify the paradigm of research you have adopted and acknowledge its limitations. Very often the researcher's own values and beliefs about how knowledge is constructed will influence the chosen paradigm. Qualitative researchers, for example, tend to place value on an individual's experiences, thoughts and feelings, whilst quantitative researchers value what is measurable. In addition, you must also explore the strengths and limitations of the chosen research methods by drawing on methodology literature. This is the very essence of what constitutes a *methodology*.

Key points

- Qualitative approaches to research are useful if you are interested in the viewpoints and feelings of your participants. However, qualitative studies tend to be small-scale and can be subjective.
- Quantitative approaches to research are useful if you are interested in identifying patterns or trends across wider samples. However, data tend to lack richness and depth, which is often achieved in qualitative studies.

Ethical issues

Grieg et al. (2007: 169) argue that 'ethics is one part of the research process that should *never* be learned in practice'. It is therefore essential that researchers have considered all the ethical implications of their research project *prior to* carrying out any research. Educational researchers have the added complexity of often using children as participants for their research. It is therefore essential that all necessary steps are taken to protect children from risk of harm. Names of children, staff and institutions should remain anonymous in all instances. This is also important even in situations where participants have declared that they do not object to their name being cited in the research report. It is argued that participants may not always be able to predict any risks that may arise as a result of publishing their names. The responsibility therefore rests with the researcher to maintain anonymity at all costs.

Student researchers must also be careful not to inadvertently reveal the identities of their participants through writing in a particular way so that the identity is obvious to the reader, even though actual names of participants have not been used. For example, 'The Year 1 teacher disagreed with some of the school policies and feels that the school lacks clear direction and leadership.' It would be obvious to anyone in the school which teacher the researcher was referring to and revealing identities in this way could jeopardize people's careers. Therefore, it is advised that researchers are more cautious in their use of language when findings are being written up.

Consent

Researchers need to gain *informed consent* from their participants prior to commencing the research. The principle of informed consent is based on the premise that participants should be given full information about the aims and purposes of the research prior to them agreeing to participate. Cohen et al. (2000) argue that informed consent has four elements: competence; voluntarism; full information; and comprehension. It is vital that individuals are responsible and mature and able to make decisions on the basis of information given (*competence*). An individual with a psychological impairment would be an example of someone who is unable to fulfil this requirement. The research participant should not be coerced into taking part. They should do this voluntarily with full awareness of any risks involved (*voluntarism*). All participants should be aware of the aims and purposes of the research and have knowledge of how the data will be used (*full information*). Finally, participants should fully understand the nature of the research project and understand the situation they are putting themselves into, before agreeing to take part (*comprehension*).

The concept of informed consent also applies to children as participants of research projects. Grieg et al. (2007) stress that it is important that both the child and adults with parental responsibility are made aware of the aims and implications of the research. They argue that consent should be obtained from both parties (if it is appropriate for the child to give their consent) and that children should know that they could choose whether to participate and have the right to withdraw from the research at any time without putting themselves at risk. In addition, the authors stress that children have the right to know what will happen to the data which are generated from the research.

Permission to gain access to institutions, schools and classrooms is essential but Grieg et al. argue that informed consent should be considered prior to gaining access. This is because the *gatekeepers* (those people who have a responsibility to *safeguard* the participants, for example, the headteacher) may ask researchers how they intend to gain permission from parents, carers and children. Therefore the researcher will need to think through issues related to informed consent prior to approaching the gatekeepers. The gatekeepers may wish to check the research tools such as questionnaires or interview schedules prior to them being used on participants. The gatekeepers should advise on whether written consent is needed from participants and parents, and universities and other HEIs will also have their own policies on this. It is vital that researchers follow the ethical procedures laid down by their own university as well as conforming to the ethical procedures demanded by the gatekeepers of the research institution.

Confidentiality

Researchers also need to think through issues related to confidentiality. It is important that promises of confidentiality are upheld. Kimmel (1988) notes that assurances of confidentiality need to be clear and potential respondents have an expectation that confidentiality will be protected. Interviews with adults should generally be carried out in a private room and the discussion should be confined to the limits of those four walls. Researchers need to think about how collected data will be stored safely and whether 'raw' data (tape recordings, field notes) will be destroyed at the end of the research. However, educational research is often not so simple. For example, ethical issues may arise during the research, especially in cases where participants reveal information which the researcher is concerned about. Sometimes, in situations like this, promises of confidentiality can only be tentative. Schools may also insist that interviews with children are not carried out in private. This is increasingly likely in the current context on safeguarding children. Thus, a member of staff may need to be present during the data collection process and this could skew the results. Some children may not talk as openly in front of their teachers as they would do to a 'researcher' who is not connected to the school and parents may not talk openly to teacher-researchers carrying out research within their own institutions. Researchers may already be employed in the school and so these issues may not arise but teacher-researchers researching within their own institution need to be aware that power relationships will be operating and that children may not feel comfortable in being entirely honest with their teachers. Researchers carrying out research in a different institution have the advantage that they can claim to be a 'researcher' rather than a 'teacher'. This might create more of an equal relationship between the participant and the researcher.

These examples from Case study C show the issues of ethics have been addressed within the methodology sections:

> Whether a small- or large-scale project, it is important as both a researcher and a professional that ethical issues are addressed. Failure to do so would not only compromise research but could also compromise the professional position of a practitioner. Burton and Bartlett (2005) refer to *The Ethical Guidelines for Educational Research* by the British Research Association (BERA 2003) and from these infer that there are five key issues that teacher researchers should be concerned with, namely <u>consent; honesty and openness; access to findings; researcher effects; and anonymity.</u>

Exercise 4.1

Consider how you might ensure that each of the underlined areas was properly addressed. Once you have noted these, check what this researcher did by reading the text from Case study A:

Hendricks (2006: 110) recognizes that ethical guidelines 'protect the rights of human subjects/participants' and 'ensure that participants are not harmed or deceived, that they have been informed regarding what participation entails, that they have agreed to participate, and that they have been assured that confidentiality of their responses and their participation will be maintained'. As well as the ethical issues surrounding the questionnaire discussed earlier in the chapter there were other ethical considerations.

Exercise 4.2

What other ethical issues do you think were faced? How would you overcome them? Refer to Part 3 of Case study C.

Key points

- Check the HEI policy on ethical procedures and ensure that you follow them carefully.
- Identify who the gatekeepers are and gain the necessary permission from them before you start your research.
- Explain the aims and purposes of your research clearly to any participants and explain what you will do with any data that you collect during the course of the study. Emphasize to your participants that their involvement remains voluntary at all times and that they have the right to withdraw at any stage during the research.
- Ensure that you maintain anonymity and uphold promises of confidentiality unless this puts others at risk of harm.

Action research

Many teacher-researchers will be operating within a short cycle of action research. Grieg et al. (2007: 136) define action research as 'a continuous learning process in which new knowledge is both learned and also shared with those who may benefit from it'. Action research focuses on reflecting on practice and improving teaching and learning through developing interventions, which seek to solve the inherent problems within institutions and classrooms. Action research can also improve the quality of education for individuals or groups of learners by modifying existing practices within classrooms. Therefore action research seeks to transform practice. It draws on both qualitative and quantitative methods but:

> enshrouds many of the basic principles of qualitative research in that it is carried out in natural, real world settings, is participatory, constructs theory from practice, involves dynamic processes of change as it progresses and aims for understanding of meaning and experience.
>
> (Ibid.: 136)

It is important that researchers justify their choice of method/s and acknowledge the strengths and limitations of each method.

In Case study C, the general aims are stated as:

> In this small-scale research project, the practitioner wanted to improve her own practice through reflection and find a starting point for collaborative enquiry ... The practitioner hoped to further her own professional development and begin a 'reflective dialogue' in the setting by discussing research findings with colleagues.

Exercise 4.3

Consider how the researcher might have therefore justified the use of action research, then read Section 3.1 of Case study C.

Some of the research methods used in action research are summarized below.

Case studies

In Case study research the student must first of all define the 'case' to be studied. A case could be one school, one classroom, one individual, one local authority or one country. Therefore 'case' is not necessarily synonymous with small-scale studies. A major criticism of Case study research is that of generalizability, although Denscombe (1998) argues that cases can be generalized if the example used in the Case study is similar to others of its type. Case studies can draw upon a range of research methods such as observation, interviews, focus groups and questionnaires.

Observations

Observations can take many forms from structured to unstructured, be participant or non-participant. Bell (2005) provides a very useful overview of this method of research and she gives examples of observation schedules. Researchers considering this method need to be aware that this method requires considerable skill in being able to 'spot significant events' (Nisbet 1977: 15). This method of research is useful in that it enables researchers to observe people in their natural context. However, this method is highly subjective since observers will filter material obtained from an observation and impose their own interpretations on what is being observed (Bell 2005). Bell recommends joint observations as a way of reducing subjectivity and bias in the research process.

Thus in the methodology section of Case study C:

> Observations were used to gather data for this study. An open observation approach was used, as using a structured observation schedule would impose structure at an early stage and restrict the data collected (Brown and Dowling 1998). A preferred method was to make more general, ethnographic observations so that different interpretations and foci would be possible, incidents could be related and emerging trends explored (Hopkins 1998).

Interviews

Researchers who choose to use interviews as a research tool will need to decide which type of interview to use. Interviews can be highly structured, such as those used in market research, where there is no deviation from the questions and the questions are asked in a fixed order. Semi-structured interviews are popular and tend to be more flexible than structured interviews. According to Hitchcock and Hughes:

> The semi-structured interview is a much more flexible version of the structured interview ... it allows depth to be achieved by providing the opportunity on the part of the interviewer to probe and expand the respondent's responses.

(1995: 157)

Semi-structured interviews therefore offer the potential of providing rich data and allow the respondents some control in determining the direction of the research. This is because they are flexible and allow the researcher to deviate from the interview schedule in order to follow up participants' responses. The participant controls the agenda for unstructured interviews to an even greater extent. However, interviews can be time-consuming and analysis of responses is not always easy, plus they can be highly subjective and may be biased (Bell 2005).

Questionnaires

Research students typically think of using questionnaires as a quick and efficient method of obtaining large amounts of data. However, they should approach the task of designing a questionnaire with caution. Good questionnaires are not easy to design; they can be costly and yield low return rates. According to Grieg et al.:

> Questionnaires are among the most common method used by researchers – and the worst carried out. Bad questionnaires will effectively torpedo the whole project, no matter how much labour is expended ... Many of these questionnaires seem to have been sent out when, for all practical purposes, they were still at their first draft. There is only one place for the first draft of any questionnaire – the bin. If you ignore this advice, your project will probably end up there instead.

> (2007: 124)

Cohen et al. (2000) provide some invaluable guidance on developing questionnaires which incorporate Likert scales (devised by R. Likert in 1932). These ask respondents to indicate their response to a statement on a numerical scale (for example: 'School is fun': 5 = strongly agree; 4 = agree; 3 = neither agree nor disagree; 2 = disagree; 1 = strongly disagree). However, scales can vary between three, five and seven points (Bell 2005). Questions of this nature make analysis easier but careful wording is needed to ensure that statements are not ambiguous. Ranking scales can also be used where respondents are asked to rank a set of statements into order of importance. Questions can be open-ended such as 'What are your views on ...?' to more closed types such as Boolean questions (where there are two responses and the choice of one automatically precludes the other, such as male/female or yes/no responses). A good questionnaire will probably include a range of different types of questions.

It is crucial that questionnaires are piloted first with a critical friend and it is always advisable for research students to let their supervisor look at a copy of a draft questionnaire prior to sending it out. If postal questionnaires are being used, it is courteous to send a cover letter outlining the purposes of the research and an explanation of how the data will be used. A stamped addressed envelope is also necessary if you want a good return rate. In some instances it may be possible for you to use questionnaires already published but this obviously depends on the nature of the research project. Bell (2005) provides a very useful overview of the pitfalls to avoid when designing questionnaires, for example, avoiding double questions, leading questions and hypothetical questions.

Focus groups

Cohen et al. (2000) define focus groups as:

> a form of group interview, though not in the sense of a backwards and forwards between interviewer and group. Rather, the reliance is on the interaction within the group who discuss a topic supplied by the researcher.

> (2000: 288)

Focus groups have a number of distinct advantages over individual interviews. They are economical on time and allow a significant amount of data to be collected from a large number of participants in a relatively short period of time (Wilkinson 2004; Cohen et al. 2000). Wilkinson argues that one of the advantages of using focus groups over individual interviews is that they are more 'naturalistic' in the sense that they resemble ordinary conversations. This is important because in these contexts people generally feel more relaxed and are therefore more willing to express their views in front of others. Stewart and Shamdasani have argued that focus group interactions create a 'synergistic effect' (1990: 16). This refers to the process of participants reacting and building on the responses of other group members. Wilkinson (2004) argues that this process helps to produce more elaborated accounts than those which are often generated in individual interviews. According to Madriz, 'the interaction in focus groups emphasizes empathy and commonality of experiences and fosters self-disclosure and self-validation' (1998: 116). Another advantage of focus groups over individual interviews is the participants may not always agree with each other. Kitzinger writes 'they also misunderstand one another, question one another, try to persuade each other of the justice of their point of view and sometimes they vehemently disagree (1994: 170–1).

However, focus groups have been criticized in the literature. It has been argued that focus groups can result in the marginalization of minority opinions or opposing points of view (Gordon and Langmaid 1988). Some writers have also criticized focus groups by arguing that group dominance by strong personalities and pressurizing conformity are often features of these sessions (McDonald 1993; Ulmenstein 1995).

Listening to the pupils' voice

The Every Child Matters agenda (2003) and the Children Act (2004) place great emphasis on the importance of listening to the voice of the child. Collecting the views of learners can be very useful in action research in terms of whether interventions have been successful. Pupil voice can also help to cast light on key issues within educational establishments from their perspective. Pupils can be consulted through a range of research tools, including focus groups, individual interviews, observations and questionnaires. Formal interviews may be inappropriate and threatening for young children and informal conversations may be better. The age and maturity of the children will therefore influence the research method.

ICT-Based Research Methods

The use of ICT has made research easier. A wealth of information is now available to you. It is possible to search for electronic journal articles and electronic books from the comfort of the study at home. The university's electronic library will be a very useful starting point. University libraries subscribe to various journals and publishers and it is possible to obtain peer-reviewed texts free of charge. However, it is still recommended that you visit the library and thumb through the literature on the shelves, as this is quite a satisfying task in itself. You should aim for a balanced list of sources in your list of references and there should not be an over-use of web-based material (see Chapter 2).

Computer software is now available for analysing qualitative data. However, you should remember that feeding data into a computer package could result in not having a 'feel' for the data, even though this method may save time. Generally, you should seek advice from tutors on whether they recommend this approach to analysis.

Exercise 4.4

Look at the following extract from Case study C.

Research performed in the 1920s and 1930s (cited in Roethlis-berger and Dickinson, 1939) into working conditions found that subjects can perform differently due to the fact that they are part of research, known as the *Hawthorne effect*.

- How might the Hawthorne effect influence other types of research, for example, questionnaire research, or research using semi-structured interviews?
- Think of a situation where you are in a leadership position and you are carrying out research with participants who work within your team. To what extent might your role as a leader influence your research findings and how can the influence of power on these findings be minimized?

Key points

- Choose the methods which best address the aims of your research.
- Justify your chosen methods in the methodology chapter but also acknowledge their limitations.

Piloting your data collection instruments

It is important that you trial your research tools prior to using them. Careful piloting can reveal issues such as leading questions and confusing questions in questionnaires and interview schedules. Piloting can also help you to predict what reaction your respondents might give to particular questions.

Exercise 4.5

In Case study A, the researcher states:

Piloting the research methods has several functions including improving the likelihood that the data collected will be reliable, valid and collect the information expected (Cohen et al. 2000), therefore each research method was piloted.

How did the researcher ensure that her research instruments were piloted on different audiences? How did she ensure that the audiences who participated in the pilot were similar to the real samples used in the actual study? (You may need to refer to p. 160.)

Data collection

You need to give careful consideration as to how you collect qualitative data. Interviews can be tape-recorded and later transcribed, although this is a very time-consuming process and respondents may object to being recorded. Instead you may choose to make notes whilst they are carrying out the interview, although this can impede the quality of the interaction between the researcher and the participants and could also result in loss of data. In short, there is no perfect mechanism for collecting data. Research diaries and logs are useful methods of collecting data, particularly for noting critical incidents.

Data analysis

You also need to think about how you intend to analyse the data when you are designing research instruments (e.g. questionnaires, interview schedules). Research tools should be designed to make data analysis as simple as possible. Miles and Huberman (1984) point out that qualitative data come in the form of words rather than numbers. Tape recordings can be transcribed and transcripts can then be coded into emerging themes. The analysis chapter can then be organized into these themes and the findings can be discussed in relation to literature.

Typically, you will find the analysis chapter the hardest to write. Students sometimes present their data question by question (in the case of questionnaire research) and this makes for very tedious reading. Instead, it is better to present a reduced form of the data where interesting patterns, regularities or irregularities have been identified. This will produce a much richer discussion. Findings need to be discussed but related to literature. Therefore it is not enough simply to state that '87 per cent of boys hated reading'. This needs to be discussed in relation to research studies and wider literature on the topic. You can relate findings to earlier sources of literature previously cited in your literature review, for example, the findings might concur or contrast with the studies and viewpoints that have already been documented. Sometimes findings may throw up something interesting, which has not been acknowledged in the literature review. Therefore, in these instances it will be necessary for the research student to look at other literature to see if similar findings have been documented. The best pieces of research will produce findings that are original, i.e. findings that have not been documented in literature, although this will be rare.

Research diary

A research diary is a useful way of demonstrating the research process to a supervisor, of recording any problems, which were encountered during the research, or any changes which needed to be made. An example of a research diary is shown in Figure 4.1:

Month	Action to be taken	Work to be completed
February 2006	• Meet with supervisor to discuss the aims of the research and the content of the literature review. • Start background reading. • Contact Case study school and obtain permission to carry out the research.	• By end of February complete introduction to dissertation.
March 2006	• Meet with supervisor to discuss the proposed methods of data collection and ethical issues. • Email interview schedules to supervisor for comment. Amend if necessary.	• By end of March complete the Literature Review.

April 2006	• At the beginning of April start reading literature on methodology. • Pilot the focus group schedule. • **Spend 5 days in Case study school.** Carry out observations in Case study school and complete interviews with key informants.	• By mid April complete the Methodology chapter.
May 2006	• Listen to the interview data. Make notes from the tape recordings.	**Start results/analysis chapter:** • Write up key findings from interview data. • Write up key findings from observations in Case study school.
June 2006	• Meet with supervisor to discuss analysis of data.	**End June:** • Complete results/ analysis chapter
July 2006	• Meet with supervisor to discuss conclusions. • Final proof reading. • Binding.	• Write conclusions to the study. • Submit finished dissertation.

Figure 4.1 A research diary

Extended project

Form a discussion group with other students on your course. Take your research proposal to the meetings and allow other members of the group to question you about aspects of your study, with a particular focus on the methodology. Allow group members to help you think through your methods. Take your research instruments to the meetings and pilot them on the rest of the group.

Key points

- Think carefully about how you will collect your data. Tape recordings provide an accurate record of discussions but they

are time-consuming to transcribe. Field notes are more time efficient but there is potential for data loss.
- Always ask your participants for permission to tape-record their conversations.
- Design your research instruments to make data analysis easier.

References

Bell, J. (2005) *Doing Your Research Project: A Guide for First-Time Researchers in Education, Health and Social Science*, 4th edn. Maidenhead: Open University Press.

Bryman, A. (1988) *Quantity and Quality in Social Research*. London: Unwin Hyman.

Clough, P. and Nutbrown, C. (2002) *A Student's Guide to Methodology*. London: Sage.

Cohen, L. Manion, L. and Morrison, K. (2000) *Research Methods in Education*, 5th edn. London: Routledge Falmer.

Denscombe, M. (1998) *The Good Research Guide for Small-Scale Social Research Projects*. Buckingham: Open University Press.

Denzin, N. and Lincoln, Y. (eds) (2000) *Handbook of Qualitative Research*, 2nd edn. Thousand Oaks, CA: Sage.

Gordon, W. and Langmaid, R. (1988) *Qualitative Market Research*. Aldershot: Gower.

Grieg, A., Taylor, J. and Mackay, T. (2007) *Doing Research with Children*, 2nd edn. London: Sage.

Habermas, J. (1972) *Knowledge and Human Interests*, trans. J. Shapiro. London: Heinemann.

Hampden-Turner, C. (1970) *Radical Man*. Cambridge, MA: Schenkman.

Hargreaves, D. (1996), Teaching as a research-based profession: possibilities and prospects, Teacher Training Agency Annual Lecture, London.

Hitchcock, G. and Hughes, D. (1995) *Research and the Teacher: A Qualitative Introduction to School-Based Research*. London: Routledge.

Holloway, I. (1997) *Basic Concepts for Qualitative Research*. Oxford: Blackwell.

Kimmel, A.J. (1988) *Ethics and Values in Applied Social Research.* Beverly Hills, CA: Sage.

Kitzinger, J. (1994) The methodology of focus groups: The importance of interaction between research participants, *Sociology of Health and Illness,* 16: 103–121.

Madriz (1998), in P. Clough and C. Nutbrown (2002) *A Student's Guide to Methodology.* London: Sage.

McDonald, W.J., (1993) Focus group research dynamics and reporting: an examination of research objectives and moderator influences, *Journal of the Academy of Marketing Science,* 12, 161–8.

Miles, M. and Huberman, A. (1984) *Qualitative Data Analysis.* London: Sage.

Nisbet, J.D. (1977) Small-scale research: guidelines and suggestions for development, *Scottish Educational Studies,* 9: 13–17.

Roszak, T. (1970) *The Making of a Counter Culture.* London: Faber and Faber.

Richardson, J. (ed.) (1996) *Handbook of Qualitative Research Methods for Psychology and the Social Sciences.* Leicester: BPS Books.

Silverman, D. (2000) *Doing Qualitative Research: A Practical Handbook.* London: Sage.

Stewart and Shamdasani (1990), in D. Silverman (ed.) (2004) *Qualitative Research: Theory, Method and Practice.* London: Sage.

Tooley, J. (1998) *Educational Research – A Critique: A Survey of Published Educational Research.* London: Ofsted.

Ulmenstein, C. von. (1995) Beyond demographics: qualitative breakthroughs in South Africa, in K. Ruyter (1996) Focus versus nominal group interviews: A comparative analysis, *Marketing, Intelligence and Planning,* 14(6): 44–50.

Wilkinson, S. (2004) Focus group research, in D. Silverman (ed.) *Qualitative Research: Theory, Method and Practice.* London: Sage.

5 Methods of evaluation

One always dies unsure of one's own value and that of one's works. Virgil himself, as he lay dying, wanted the *Aeneid* burning.

(Gustave Flaubert, *Letter to Louise Colet*, 1852)

Introduction

This chapter defines evaluation and explores formative and summative approaches to it. It considers the role of the researcher in ensuring validity, reliability and research objectivity. It defines triangulation and outlines why data and evidence must be treated with caution. It then seeks to analyse the ways in which both practitioner and learner voices can be used to help you to evaluate.

What is an evaluation?

An evaluation attempts to assess, or measure the value of something. Notice the word 'value'. The value given to something is determined by what the teacher-researcher values, or often what the organization funding or promoting the evaluation values. To consider if something is 'value for money', for example suggests that any outcomes from an educational activity can be measured in terms of the money value generated from a money input. Some might consider such a measure of educational value to be inappropriate, while others might consider it essential. So, we need to ask, who is doing the evaluation, why they are doing it, and finally, how? First, we will consider who is doing the evaluation.

An evaluation of a lesson, or a programme, or unit of work is underpinned by a need. The point to consider is whose need? If it is the need of the practitioner, then clearly the needs of the learner and their values may be largely ignored. Is this appropriate for an educational evaluation? Often, you will take into account the values of the learners who are the focus for your research. If the focus of the research is that of other practitioners, then their values must be taken into account if an appropriate method of evaluation is to be used.

If certification is an important value to those who are the focus of the evaluation, then some form of 'outcome' measurement will be required. In this case a quantitative method might be appropriate. If a more intrinsic value, such as pleasure or curiosity in learning is considered important, then a more qualitative approach must be taken. An evaluation is not an impartial measurement of the worth of something. It is laden with values, values that are often hidden. The good researcher will make these values clear at the beginning of an evaluation.

Summative or formative?

If a *summative* approach to evaluation is taken, this may be at the end of a research project. This would often be a claim to some new insight into the nature of knowledge or methodology. This is a big claim to make. It is likely that you will be involved in a small-scale piece of work, maybe focusing on your own practice. In this instance is it more appropriate to take a *formative* approach to evaluation. You will write about provisional findings or implications rather than conclusions. You should suggest ways in which research could be conducted in the future, either by you, or somebody else, in order to improve the quality of the research you have done or to explore other issues that you now find at the end of your work are important.

Second, we need to ask why we need to evaluate. This will help us to determine how we evaluate. The tool of evaluation must be fit for the purpose it was designed for. For example, if we want to know *why* certain learners will not engage with a piece of work, then a practitioner's lesson evaluation that relies upon observed behaviour of a group of learners is unlikely to offer valid insight into why this is happening. If we want to know *if* learners are engaging with a piece of work, then this form of observation may provide a starting point, or offer one perspective. They may appear to be engaging. But we would need to dig deeper by using another evaluation tool, maybe documentary evidence, such as a learner's work, or an interview that explores an observed critical incident. We shall be looking at some of these evaluation tools when we consider triangulation.

The evidence we present must support the claims that we are making for it. This takes us to the idea of *validity*. For example, how do we know that learners are engaging with the concepts we are teaching? What is the link between what we claim and the evidence that we have? Does observation of behaviour really tell us much about engagement with concepts? In some instances it could offer some insight, in other instances we might simply be observing 'busyness'. What sort of observation would be valid? What would we need to be looking for?

If we argue that our claims are valid, then colleagues and others who are interested must be able to see the link between the evidence and our claim. If you are presenting evidence from small-scale research, then there is always a suggestion of bias, or that you have distorted the results in some way. Your research can never be completely objective. Rather than denying this it is wise to acknowledge the possibility and take reasonable steps to reduce your influence. In this chapter, for example, the use of language like 'outcome' or 'pleasure in learning' in themselves indicates a 'bias', or less pejoratively, a 'perspective' on learning. Similarly, you need to recognize that your own values influence the choice of evaluation method, and the significance you read into the results. Steps can be taken to reduce the impact of such a perspective (inviting others to suggest methods of evaluation and to join you in the analysis) but you cannot take the researcher completely out of the research. Something you could do is to openly express your interest in this issue at the beginning of your piece of research, so readers can make their own mind up about the significance of the research. If the reader understands your perspective, then he sees if the inferences that you make are valid.

Inference

If you want your learners to engage in the concepts you are teaching, then you need to ensure that your reader understands how you have reached your conclusion. Sometimes, a practitioner will bring insight that a non-practitioner would not have. So, to return to our example of observation, two teachers observing a discussion group would identify the language used by a group of learners in a class discussion as evidence of critical engagement with the desired concepts. A non-practitioner may simply see a group of people talking 'round a subject' and may consider some of the discussion trivial, or miss the point entirely. Inference is valid if those who share your cultural perspective, in this case, the perspective of a practitioner, can see the same things in the data.

Key points

- In Masters Level work it is advisable to use formative evaluation. Use your evaluation as feedback that is used to inform future practice or research.

- Knowledge is often provisional. This means that it is unlikely that you can prove that something works. It is simply the case that no one has yet disproved what you have found, or, that they haven't yet found a better way, but they will eventually, or maybe you will, when you try out some of the ideas that you have explored in your Masters Level work.

Validity and reliability

Qualitative research can be charged with a lack of rigour and bias (Charmaz 2001). The reason for this is that meaning and interpretation require inference that is not shared by all. This is another reason why an evaluation needs to clearly state the 'who, why and how' of the evaluation. Answering these questions indicates the cultural perspective you are drawing upon for inference. Those who share your perspective, or understand it, can judge if your inferences are valid, and those who do not share your cultural perspective can at least see how you have arrived at your evaluation.

Whilst Charmaz (2001) asserts that validity, truth and generalizability are 'outmoded concepts', it is not argued here that validity and reliability should be removed from the methodology. However, educational research methods require the building of trust and empathy – sometimes called *rapport* – between the informant and the researcher. This undermines the claim of the educational researcher that there is reliability of method, that is, that another researcher can take your research tool and obtain the same data. The social situation of teaching and learning is dynamic and dependent upon relationships. The researcher cannot remove all elements of human reaction, and indeed this is unwise as it may lead to defensiveness and a response that produces 'thin' data – data that offer limited insight into the issues being explored. There has to be a compromise between reliability and validity in order to generate meaningful, insightful data.

Exercise 5.1

Is the inference evident in this extract from Case study C valid?

Harry did not seem to become as distressed as often or as severely during the study as the practitioner had observed on previous occasions, Harry can often be more distressed after the school holidays when returning to nursery. Perhaps a long-term study would truly reflect the effectiveness of the schedule. A criticism of this study may be that it is difficult to define 'distress' and one observer's opinion may differ markedly from another, making this study difficult to repeat.

Rapport

Rapport provides better quality data and improves your claims to validity. However, it undermines reliability as you are unlikely to have the same rapport with a range of practitioners and learners, and it is also unlikely that another researcher can develop the same rapport. This makes it difficult to replicate your data collection method. A balance therefore needs to be struck between validity and reliability. A semi-structured interview or observation schedule – a schedule with key headings – is the compromise that many educational researchers use. This schedule is then used to frame observations or interviews with a number of informants. This structure should allow for similar data to be generated with a range of informants, and a range of researchers.

Triangulation

Triangulation is a way of checking your data against that obtained from another evaluation tool. If the same issues are found in different methods of data collection, this will increase the validity of your claims. It is also a chance to investigate an issue more deeply (see Chapter 3 on progressive focusing).

Some of the issues you need to take account of when using different evaluation tools to collect data are considered here. Some of the points made under headings, such as those for interviewing, might well apply to other methods. There is a fine balance between rapport and validity, and bias and unreliability. In your evaluation methods you need to be aware of these issues, try and get the balance right and take as many precautions as is reasonable to address issues of bias and unreliability. Triangulation will help, but integrity and an audit trail will also contribute. In other words, you must make it clear where the supporting evidence for your claims come from: which interview, lesson plan or observation? Good quality data, faithfully recorded and attributed to the findings in your evaluation will go a long way to repel any attacks upon the validity and reliability of your research.

The practitioner's voice

One important source of data is the practitioner's voice because of its potential to reveal what happens in the heart of the learning situation. But, there are a number of problems associated with the practitioner's voice.

be underestimated. University students (and lecturers) do not find it easy. Academic work will show varying degrees of criticality from the start of the programme through to completion. Masters Level programmes usually culminate in the submission of an extended piece of academic writing, such as a dissertation. It is crucial that this work evidences a substantial level of critical and reflective thinking in order for students to complete the course successfully. In other words, you will need to demonstrate to the reader that you have developed sufficient understanding of the area of study to develop your own authoritative voice. The ability to demonstrate *mastery* of the topic is therefore crucial to success.

Evidence of 'mastery' of the topic will be achieved by being critical. The author will have read a very wide range of literature and explored the contrasting arguments in relation to the key debates. He/She will have developed enough knowledge of the topic, to the extent that they can challenge viewpoints in the literature with contrasting viewpoints. The author will have demonstrated the ability to synthesize these contrasting viewpoints by making a case to support the validity of one argument over another and will have demonstrated an ability to relate the topic to wider theories and theoretical frameworks and to question the assumptions made by these.

However, it is important to emphasize that critical thinking is not just about criticizing viewpoints in the literature, criticizing government policies or criticizing practice, although this is part of it! Television and theatre critics encourage us to view criticality in a negative sense. 'Criticality' originates from the Greek *krisis*, which means 'a sifting'. Therefore part of your job will be to sift through the text and identify the aspects which are good or poor. Thinking in a critical and reflective manner is also about acknowledging the strengths of viewpoints in the literature and the strengths of theories and theoretical frameworks. Therefore, the aim should be to identify not just contrasting opinions in the literature but also concurring opinions and viewpoints.

Balance

Your aim should be to produce a balanced discussion, which examines both sides of the arguments in relation to the key debates. For example, a paper on inclusive education could explore the arguments for and against segregated special education. The writer would read widely in the literature and find viewpoints from academics in support of segregated education for children with Special Educational Needs. In addition, the writer would find viewpoints in the literature from academics who disagree with the notion of segregated education. To explore the contrasting viewpoints in the literature the writer might find a colour-coding system useful with arguments for segregated education highlighted in one colour and arguments against highlighted in another. This will be done across several books/journal articles. This process will help the writer to compare viewpoints from across the literature. The writer would present both sides of the debate through citing the contrasting viewpoints. Finally, the writer would synthesize these contrasting viewpoints by arguing a case for/against segregated education. A good starting point, therefore, is to identify the key debates within the topic/field that is being studied.

Key points

- None of the skills identified here are easy, nor do they necessarily come naturally.
- Reflect on the viewpoints that you cite from the literature. Are they logical or valid? Can you challenge them?
- Explore the criticisms of key theories and theoretical frameworks.
- Always aim to present a balanced viewpoint by exploring opposing arguments.

Types of criticality

Presenting contrasting points of view

The aim here is for you to identify contrasting viewpoints in the literature. In order to do this effectively it will be necessary for you to read widely first. Books and journal articles are always good starting points as these sources have usually been peer-reviewed or refereed. (For caveats regarding literature, see Chapter 2.) Newspaper articles from reputable newspapers (such as the *Guardian* or the *Times Education Supplement*) will also prove to be valuable. Increasingly, university students are using web-based sources, although over-use of web-based material is not advisable due to the fact that it often has not been subject to academic scrutiny. Electronic journals, newspaper articles and electronic books will be available via the university's electronic database. However, there is nothing more satisfying than actually visiting the library and searching the shelves in person! Chapter 2 details possible sources and their advantages and disadvantages.

How much do you need to read?

It will be necessary to draw the line somewhere in terms of how much material to peruse. There is always another book or another journal article that could have been read! Whilst reading the literature it will be necessary to identify key themes and debates for which a colour coding system, as described above, will be helpful. Sometimes multiple coding is necessary; for example, if you are researching sources of teacher stress several themes may be identified such as workload, work–life balance, pressure to get children to reach standards, inspection, etc. These themes will appear across several sources of literature and each should be identified using highlighter pens or coloured Post-It notes (in books). You will then be able to identify similar and contrasting viewpoints in relation to each theme across the literature.

Exercise 6.1

Read the following extract from Case study A:

> Feinstein and Symons (1999: 306) contend that 'variables such as class size and teacher experience are usually found to have little effect on attainment'. This, however, does not appear to reflect the view of Ofsted (1997: 9) who state that 'there are clear links between unsatisfactory teaching and low levels of attainment' and Wright et al. (1997: 63) who state that 'the most important factor affecting students learning is the teacher'. Important is the statement by Wright et al. (1997: 63) that 'students in classrooms of very effective teachers, following relatively ineffective teachers make excellent academic gains but not enough to offset previous evidence of less than expected gains'.

The author has clearly presented two different points of view, thus demonstrating criticality. This is a particularly good example because she has supported the contrasting viewpoint (in this case, Ofsted) with a concurring viewpoint (Wright et al.). This strengthens the critique because she has added weight to the contrasting view.

Challenging a viewpoint: developing an authoritative voice

Below is a somewhat humorous summary of an *uncritical* review of the literature. The writers describe an uncritical review as:

> The furniture sale catalogue, in which everything merits a one-paragraph entry no matter how skilfully it has been conducted:

Bloggs (1975) found this, Smith (1976) found that, Jones (1977) found the other, Bloggs, Smith and Jones (1978) found happiness in heaven.

(Haywood and Wragg 1982: 2)

Clearly there is a need to go beyond mere description of viewpoints in the literature. At Masters Level you need to be able to demonstrate that you are able to engage with the viewpoints and offer some reflection upon them. This will involve the ability to question assumptions and assertions and to challenge viewpoints in the literature. Challenging viewpoints is a skill which students often find difficult. They may feel they lack the authority to do this. After all, students are not academics, they have not had their work published and they are not well known. However, education students often bring to their studies a substantial degree of practical experience. They may have worked with learners of a wide range of ages and abilities; they have had experience of working in professional contexts and they will have engaged in professional dialogue with colleagues. These rich interactions will have enabled them to formulate their views and opinions about aspects of education and it is possible to draw upon this experience to question assumptions and viewpoints in the literature. In addition, through engaging with a wide range of literature, students become more knowledgeable about the aspect of education they are studying and this gives them the confidence to question assumptions in the literature and to challenge viewpoints.

Exercise 6.2

Read the extract from Case study B carefully. Identify two places where the writer has developed an authoritative voice by questioning/ challenging viewpoints in the literature.

Building on tasks and linking explanations to prior knowledge are two further points that Kerry (1998: 108, 117) believes should be considered thoroughly when explaining. The DfES Pedagogy and Practice unit on Explaining also highlights this point:

When explaining relationships between factors we need to consider how one factor affects another ...

(DfES 2004: 3)

However, Petty emphasizes that the development of existing and new knowledge can only be advantageous in explanation when want to get the work finished and will be rushing to complete it. Often the last thing you want to do at this point is to return to the literature or carry out even more reading. However, in order to demonstrate that the work is scholarly, it is necessary to relate findings to literature.

How can students be critical at this stage of their research? Interesting data often add something new to the literature (i.e. fill a gap) or contradict it. Exploring these contradictions is a good way of demonstrating criticality.

In Case study A, findings are related to literature in a number of places:

> This statistical evidence does indicate that the background of the child does impact upon the level they achieve at the end of Key Stage 3. In subjects who are tested there is a greater difference with Mathematics showing the most significant difference between pupils from deprived backgrounds and those from relatively well off communities. This supports the findings of similar studies such as Cooper et al. (2003) who found that social deprivation is a key factor in educational underachievement.

> Figure 4.3 shows the average level achieved in ICT for pupils who are entitled to free school meals against those who do not qualify. It shows that there is a difference between the two groups with the pupils who receive free school meals attaining the lower average level. This supports the work of Smith (2003: 580) who found that 'with regard to academic variables, pupils who receive free school meals do less well than their peers in aggregate terms at every level'.

> These findings support Gorard (2000) who believed that pupils who perform well earlier in their schooling continue to do so but contradicts the work of Schagen (2006: 121) who argued that the relationship between prior attainment and performance is 'not linear'.

In this last example the author has findings which conflict with the literature. This would then form the basis of an excellent critical discussion. The author can then explain why the results are as they are and then use this as a basis for questioning or challenging the literature.

Extended project

Form a critical discussion group with other students on your course. Try to meet on a regular basis. Take articles and other texts to the meetings and have a critical discussion about the content. This will be invaluable with texts that you are using for your assignments.

Key points

- Relate your findings to literature.
- Use your data to challenge or support viewpoints in the literature.
- Evaluate the extent to which your data is original, i.e. has it produced new findings that have not been discovered before, or does it simply add to existing bodies of knowledge?

References

Armstrong, D. (2005) Reinventing 'inclusion': New Labour and the cultural politics of special education, *Oxford Review of Education*, 31(1): 135–51.

Brause, R. (2000) *Writing Your Doctoral Dissertation.* Florence, KY: Taylor and Francis.

Foucault, M. (1972) *The Archaeology of Knowledge.* London: Tavistock.

Haywood, P. and Wragg, E.D. (1982) *Evaluating the Literature,* Rediguide 2, University of Nottingham, School of Education.

Slee, R. (2001) Inclusion in practice: does practice make perfect?, *Educational Review*, 53(2): 113–23.

Part III
Written Outcomes at Masters Level

mealtimes. The strategy could be further developed to allow Harry more flexibility to be able to join children spontaneously without having to choose the card first.

The research showed that the use of a schedule helps Harry to stay on task and reduces repetitive behaviour. Although Harry's mum does not use the schedule at home to help Harry to stay on task, she does use it with success to help Harry to move on from one activity to another, as it was useful for at nursery.

(Case study C)

In an assignment that is based on a curriculum package, you could summarize the key points arising from your evaluation of the teaching and learning relating to the chosen focus.

It is clear from the above evaluation that there are many successes from teaching this unit of work with a focus on modelling and explaining. The starter listening activities provided consistency to each lesson. Explanations aided development and teacher modelling helped pupils relate to the task and actually see what they were being asked to do, as well as learning how to do it. Pupil modelling was used as an extension of this and helped to keep the class engaged; willing and wanting to take part.

(Case study B)

In this example the writer has summarized what was successful about the teaching package. In particular, she has considered the chosen focus for the assignment which in this case was teacher exposition. This example could have been enhanced further by referring specifically to samples of the evidence for the assertions made and also by referring back to appropriate literature. This is one of the key features of Gestalt, the ability to link appropriate theory to practice.

In an evidence-based practice assignment, the opening could also summarize the impact of the intervention strategy on learning and achievement. Our Case study presents an analysis of examination results showing the impact of the introduction of a new course on pupils' achievement.

The conclusions you are making here should emerge from your evaluation section or presentation of findings, and so it is important to avoid making unsubstantiated statements. You should not overstate the findings of your research or over-generalize as you try to summarizse them. Murray (2006) suggests that you can avoid using the 'over-generalising present tense' by prefacing a statement with 'This suggests that ...'. She also suggests that adding the word 'perhaps' at the beginning of a sentence also radically alters the strength of the claim you are making. It is vital that the claims you make are firmly based on the evidence presented earlier in the study.

Exercise 7.1

In this exercise you will look at one of your own assignments that you are developing. Read through your assignment and highlight the main findings that arise from your study. Identify the evidence that supports these findings. Now consider the original focus for the study or, if appropriate, the aims of the research, and make a series of statements that you can firmly support with evidence. Consider the overall 'feel' of the assignment – what message do you think it is carrying? Try to state this in a single statement or sentence. This could be something simple like 'I believe that I have shown that targeted intervention can improve learning' or 'I have investigated several ways of giving pupil feedback and can conclude that in such-and-such circumstances, this way is more effective.' This task should help you to summarize the findings and ensure that you have appropriate evidence to support the claims you will make.

Key points

- This part of the conclusion should summarize the focus of the assignment, as well as provide a brief contextual statement outlining why the study is important.
- It should summarize the key findings in relation to the aims of the research or the focus of the assignment.
- All the claims made should be firmly grounded in evidence that has been generated during the study.

Discussing impact on practice and making recommendations

Most education assignments will require you to evaluate or consider the implications of your study on classroom practice and make recommendations based on your findings. Questions that you may try to answer could be: How has the assignment led to an improved understanding of teaching and learning? What changes will I make to teaching and learning strategies as a result of the study? Campbell suggests that this section includes: 'Suggestions or reflections on what you could do differently next time, how you could further improve your intervention programme, or the costs and benefits of getting involved in teacher research' (2004: 176). These questions are particularly pertinent when writing the Conclusion for an assignment based on the teaching of a curriculum package where you will consider how the package could be improved and suggest ways in which it could be taught differently next time. You may even develop the resources further where this is asked for in the assignment. These considerations link clearly to your lesson evaluations and the evaluation section of the assignment. For example:

> As Joyce et al. (1997) state, 'the broader the range of teaching approaches ... the more likely we are to reach our goal of educating all students' (p. 25). Taking this into consideration, the best way to improve this package would be to consciously incorporate as many teaching strategies as possible, providing an amalgamation of approaches to benefit all pupils. To develop the package further it would be beneficial for pupils to actually see the instruments they are composing for, although this was not possible during this unit. Pupils' learning could also be developed by going to a live concert of Renaissance music; through my discussions with pupils during lessons it has become clear that almost all have never been to a live classical instrumental concert, an event that I believe could benefit pupils' musical appraisal, composing and listening skills dramatically. I could have developed this area further in the classroom by playing my instruments (violin and flute) in the Renaissance style and would try and integrate this if teaching the unit again.
>
> (Case study B)

For practitioners in post, this part of the Conclusion should also focus on the wider implications of your study. This might include making recommendations that involve staff and resources outside your own classroom. For example in Case study C:

> Informal observations and discussions with another teacher have shown that 'substitute' pictures (for example, using the symbol for playdough to show a cooking activity) do not work and can be more harmful than using no picture at all. It has been suggested to the special needs coordinator that the nursery could invest in a computer package that provides us with a greater number of pictures or symbols and that one person in nursery could be responsible for printing and laminating them.

The following example from Case study A makes recommendations for policy changes on a much wider level:

> The overriding factor identified in this study is that pupils' prior attainment at Key Stage 2 is directly linked to their performance at Key Stage 3. It is therefore vital that primary schools provide the best opportunities for pupils by delivering high quality teaching and learning to ensure that pupils achieve their potential. For pupils that do not make the expected progress in primary there is a real need for secondary schools to implement strategies to improve pupils' levels well before the end of KS3. This needs to take the form of targeted personalized intervention. This should mean that pupils are identified on entry to secondary school using KS2 SAT's data and information provided by the primary schools. These pupils should then be involved in a programme of high quality intervention that enhances the teaching they receive in order that they can make more progress in KS3 and achieve the national average. This in turn would lead to improvements at GCSE.
>
> The government have invested heavily in the personalization agenda recognizing that 'decisive progress in educational standards occurs where every child matters; careful attention is paid to their individual learning styles, motivations, and needs' and 'there is rigorous use of pupil target setting linked to high quality assessment' Miliband (2004: 2), but at present this appears to be having very little impact on pupils in the LA's schools. While progress is being made in some schools, it is not fast enough to benefit pupils in school now, who will be the parents of children in the LA schools in the future, continuing the cycle of deprivation. Therefore, consultant support should target these areas and support schools to implement effective intervention strategies.

Exercise 7.2

Again looking at your own assignment, list the recommendations you are making leading from your study. This will help you to organize your thoughts for this part of the Conclusion section. Note, that with assignments of this nature, that are necessarily limited in scope, there will almost always be some sort of caveat – a 'but' or a 'however' or an area or circumstance that you have been unable to investigate. Don't forget to state these limitations when making your recommendations. This shows skills of synthesis and reflection.

Dissemination and contextualization

These are two further considerations that need to be included in this part of the Conclusion section.

First, an important question that arises from making recommendations is how you will disseminate your findings. For your research to have an impact outside your own classroom, you need to create opportunities to share your work with colleagues. This could be done through informal discussion with those working closely with you, or in more formal departmental meetings, or strategically at a senior management level. Many assignments expect you to write about how you will do this. As your recommendations are implemented more widely, this may form the basis of further research.

Second, during this section of the Conclusion, it is important to contextualize your work by referring to the theories discussed in your literature review. This is an opportunity to show synthesis between theory and practice and also to answer the 'So what?' question by showing how your study has added to the field of study.

For example, in Case study A:

> In terms of making recommendations as a result of this study the problem documented by Gorard and Smith (2004: 219) that 'it is possible to identify entire groups of students with a tendency to underachieve' rings true. However, they continue that 'the category which binds then together is merely a "pseudo-explanation" for their lower achievement' and that even if they could identify the cause of the lower achievement then it is not always possible to change it. For example, in the LA it is clear from this study that the area in which a pupil lives impacts on their life chances but it is not possible for schools, local authorities or the researcher to relocate pupils to wealthier areas. However, from the findings there are opportunities to look closely at the factors impacting on KS3 ICT and try to offer ways forward for schools and the LA.

Exercise 7.3

Identify reading from your assignment which underpins your findings and contrast this with reading which possibly suggests a different view. What do your own findings add to the debate?

Key points

- The Conclusion will consider the impact of the study on your classroom practice.
- You may make recommendations for changes in policy underpinned by evidence generated during the assignment.
- An important aspect of this is how your findings and recommendations will be disseminated and developed further at a departmental and/or institutional level.
- You should place your study in context by suggesting how your findings relate to previous work in the focus area.

Avenues for further investigation and impact on professional development

During the Conclusion it is also important to consider the limitations of your study. Think about qualifications that may need to be made to your argument. For example, are there factors that have an impact on the validity or reliability of the findings of the research? You may propose a course of action or raise questions that warrant further study.

> The use of a schedule did reduce the number of times Harry was distressed at nursery although it was concluded that as Harry was distressed less than normal anyway, a longer research period would be required to truly determine the effectiveness. Harry's mum reported that she relied very much on the schedule at home to avoid distress and to help calm Harry when he was upset. However, she also spoke of times when the intervention did not work.

> (Case study C)

If working within an Action Research methodology, you may suggest the next cycle of research. For example:

> While the data collated has provided statistical data to support or disregard the factors which impact on attainment, it has not investigated the core issues in detail. For further research, a clear starting point would be to look at the issue of prior attainment at KS2 and investigate what could be done to improve the results of

pupils at eleven. Another area that requires further research is the impact of the low numbers of pupils from different ethnic groups in the authority.

The action research Case study goes as far as providing an action plan showing how the study will be continued beyond the confines of the assessed piece of work. Murray argues that a mini-proposal for future work such as this, makes for a strong ending to an assignment: 'it shows that you have sufficient expert knowledge to (a) select an appropriate priority and (b) think it through' (2006: 245).

You should then consider how the study has impacted on your personal and professional development. This might be in relation to aspects of your professional development targets or in relation to priorities inherent in your current job role. These might be also related to departmental or school improvement priorities:

> In the light of its experience with DiDA, School X chose the BTEC First Certificate as the ICT course for delivery to all year 10 students from September 2006.

> (Case study D)

In the following examples the writers discuss impact on their professional knowledge, skills and understanding:

> Personally, this study has led to a greater understanding of the wider picture of the authority and the issues it faces. It has given the researcher the confidence to discuss the issues in a wider forum and provided the statistical evidence to quantify personal beliefs about underachievement.

> (Case study A)

> This piece of action research has helped the practitioner and her colleagues to think more critically about their provision. Background research has developed a theoretical understanding of autism which have been shared with other staff to develop an understanding of the needs of children with autism. An effective intervention for Harry has been established and regular discussions with Harry's mum continue to help us to develop our provision.

> (Case study C)

The consideration of impact on your professional development is particularly important for trainee practitioners. How has your study supported your journey in meeting the standards for qualified teacher status? Which of the standards do you consider have been particularly strongly underpinned by the study? What do you need to do now to move onto the next phase of development?

For example:

> My teaching has improved considerably throughout this package and this can be seen when looking at the teacher tutor observations. Because I have had to consider my chosen teaching strategy in depth, my planning has been more consistent and I have learnt how to synthesize lessons, developing on pupils' assessed knowledge. Specifically, my explaining methods have become clearer and more focused and I have observed the benefits of teacher and pupil modelling. I am developing these strategies further now in the other modules that I teach.
>
> (Case study B)

Exercise 7.4

Think about the starting point of your investigation. What did you think you were going to gain from the investigation? What tangible personal and professional benefits have resulted from undertaking your assignment?

Key points

- During the Conclusion section it is important to consider the limitations of your study.
- This may lead to a discussion about how the investigation may be further developed.
- Describe what you have learned from undertaking the study and how this has impacted on your personal and professional development.

The closing paragraph

Finishing the assignment is perhaps the most difficult part of all to write. There are no simple answers to this. The final paragraph really depends on the assignment question. For example, in assignments that ask you to

have written, by referencing the views and practice of relevant colleagues and learners, as well as institutional policy, you will demonstrate that you fully understand the significant issues. It is important that your portfolio is grounded in a theoretical framework. Chapter 2 provides guidance for developing your literature review, and Chapter 4 for choosing methodology.

Key points

The following are guidelines for choosing a focus for a portfolio module:

- It must be something you are interested in.
- Access to the right material at M Level is important.
- It should be student-centred and be related to raising achievement and whole school development.
- Do not choose something that you are not involved with. For example, if you are not working on 'assessment for learning', however interesting you find it, you will not be able to get the right quality materials for the portfolio.
- The topic must enhance your own personal and professional development. You should feel a sense of achievement on completion of the assessment.

Methods of evaluation

It is important that you do your reading and organize your data collection at the beginning of the assessment. The submission date could seem a long way away but you must complete your evaluation with the realities and problems of the chosen area of focus. This is not easy to do 'after the event'. You can only write up and refine your evaluation when you have the relevant data/evidence to draw on if your evaluation is to be authentic and appropriate to your professional development.

There are many methods you can choose from to evaluate the focus of your portfolio. Remember, it is not the detail of the portfolio which is significant, it is the feelings, responses and attitudes which were formed from these experiences which provide the basis for the evaluation. It is important that you reflect on your reading and experiences for some time before writing your evaluation; this should help you think about how your reading has impacted on your practice.

Whatever evaluation method you choose, it must be theoretically grounded. Chapter 4 'Methodology' and Chapter 5 'Methods of evaluation' are good sources for choosing your methodology. Further guidance more specific to portfolio evaluation is outlined below:

Action research

In order to provide a critical framework in which to evaluate the portfolio you could undertake a small piece of action research. Action research is defined by McNiff and Whitehead (2006: 7) as 'a form of enquiry that enables practitioners everywhere to investigate and evaluate their work'. They assert that it is a vehicle for improving one's own learning. The action research could be quite a small project, for example, if you were 'evaluating learning and teaching' materials, you could produce a questionnaire to ask your students' views of the materials, conduct a focus group interview with students to elicit their opinions or undertake a semi-structured interview with a colleague. This will provide much richer and more objective data for the evaluation than your own opinions.

Critical incidents

One way of evaluating your portfolio is to concentrate on 'critical incidents'. These are defined by Tripp (1993: 35) as:

> Indicative of underlying trends, motives and structures ... because they provide a means of enabling teachers to be more aware of the nature of their professional values and associated problematics, to question their own practice, and to concretise their generally abstract notions of values such as social justice.

Tripp suggests that critical incidents can be identified through certain adjectives such as, silly, interesting and witty. This certainly moves away from the belief that 'critical incidents' should be quite serious events. It is very much up to the individual to define their own critical incidents in the light of what is a very personal experience. What one practitioner may regard as a critical incident may not be considered noteworthy by another.

Bell explores 'critical-incidents and problem-portfolio logs' (2005: 178–9). She cites Oxtoby (1979: 239–40) who describes this technique as an endeavour to ascertain the more 'noteworthy' aspects of job behaviour and is based on the supposition that jobs are composed of critical and non-critical tasks.

One important point that Oxtoby mentions is that this method of evaluation does not lend itself to 'objective quantification'. It is this point which makes the portfolio difficult to evaluate objectively. This is because the practitioner is evaluating a collection of materials that they have been actively engaged with. To try to present more valid evidence you could ask someone who you respect to act as 'critical friend'. McNiff and Whitehead (2006) describe this as a professional colleague, parents, client, student, or just someone who will give a valuable opinion.

Journal

Keeping a journal record of your perceptions of how the focus of your portfolio has progressed is an acceptable method of evaluating the materials. This should focus on relevance, progression, engagement and differentiation but could also include some personal reflection on critical incidents. Your learners could also be asked to keep a journal of the sessions as this is a way of triangulating the data collected. However, Knight (2002: 118) reminds us that self-reports are not always reliable, so any evidence from this source should be triangulated with other methods. Again, the critical friend can be vital.

Observation records

If you have been observed undertaking part of the tasks for the portfolio, it is a good source of evaluation evidence. This could be a lesson observation and it is important that the observer uses a 'formal observation form' to make sure it is a structured observation. Brown and Dowling (1998: 50) outline the Flanders' Interaction Analysis Categories which are useful for the classification of verbal interaction in the classroom. The observer could be a 'critical friend', 'colleague' or 'member of your senior management team'. It is important that you brief them carefully before the observation to ensure that they focus on relevant issues and are fully conversant with the observation schedule.

Video/DVD/CD

The use of video as evidence is a helpful way of providing evidence within the performing arts. You could use this to analyse the performance at a later stage. Following the conventions for observation gives it more credibility in terms of the reliability of the evidence. The use of a critical friend, again, would help to validate your views. However, remember that it is very time-consuming for a person assessing the portfolio to view or listen to lengthy video and audio material, so ideally it should be used for your own observations. Do discuss this with your tutors before embarking on this method of evaluation. There are critical issues when filming children and young people so make sure you are aware of these and adhere to recomendations.

Exercise 8.2

Select three methods of evaluation and write a list of advantages and disadvantages of using the method.

Key points

- Organize your data collection at the beginning of the assessment.
- Theoretically underpin your evaluation methodology.
- Triangulate your evaluation by using more than one method of data collection.
- Make use of a critical friend.

Accreditation

Many HEIs are prepared to offer accreditation for such qualifications which involve portfolio development as the National Professional Qualification for Headship (NPQH) and Leading from the Middle (LftM), particularly those that are members of the Universities Council for Education of Teachers (UCET). A national tariff has been agreed and for NPQH, for example, practitioners can get 60 credits and for a LftM, 30 credits. However, these qualifications are not at M Level, therefore, to gain the credit, it is necessary to undertake an evaluation of the work undertaken for the qualification.

Presentation

The portfolio should be presented in a professional file, either A4 or lever-arch, with the use of divider cards to separate the different elements. An example of this is:

The whole of the critical review could be divided into the sections indicated below. Extracts from the portfolio are given at each stage to enable you to understand the requirements.

Introduction (500 words)

Outline the rationale for choosing the particular theme for the focus of the portfolio and assignment:

> DiDA is a paperless e-qualification from Edexcel that focuses on the practical application of technology at KS4. Their website accessed 8.3.2007 states that it is "designed to 'stimulate students' creativity and develop real-world, practical skills that will motivate learning across a wide range of subjects".
>
> The school had to make a choice between 4, 2 or 1 GCSE equivalent as DiDA was seen to be replacing ICT GNVQ. Learners could, therefore, study DiDA in Year 9, most likely at Level 1, then study 2 units at Level 2 in Year 10 and one unit in Year 11.
>
> As a teacher new to secondary schools it was a big responsibility. The question was – would DiDA be a suitable ICT qualification for our students? Would it engage and motivate as the awarding body predicted and would the outcome contribute to school improvement in terms of its Value Added score?

Briefly and anonymously describe the contexts in terms of the departmental and school settings in which you have developed your practice in relation to the chosen focus:

> The writer's role at school X is a teacher of ICT at KS 3 & 4 with responsibility for leading the DiDA course. She had previously been employed as a lecturer at the local Further Education (FE) college. As a result of this position she was offered a place on the local council's Graduate Teacher Programme (GTP) and subsequently achieved Qualified Teacher Status (QTS).

Examine the key features of the portfolio and the critical factors affecting its completion:

> The achievement and attainment of pupils in all schools are published each year by the Department for Education and Skills (DfES). The league tables are key indicators of school performance and not only provide information to parents and the general public but they also ensure that schools are accountable for their results.
>
> For the purpose of this portfolio assessment the focus will be on KS4 tables which contain the results for GCSEs and equivalent

qualifications. The tables do not, however, provide results or value added for every subject taken at KS4.

Exercise 8.4

Consider which other aspects of the DiDA course the practitioner could have chosen to focus on. Do you think she made the right choice of focus?

Literature review (1000 words)

An investigation of the key texts related to the focus of the assignment:

> In this instance the student has focused on 'Value Added measures' comparing different data analysis tools which enable schools to examine context, attainment and value added data.

Include references to academic literature, regulatory and official documents and professional literature:

> Literature which has been referred to includes text books, journal articles, web references, BBC News website, DfES website materials, Edexcel documentation.

Engage in analysis and critical reflection.

> The analysis and critical reflection is based on the positive and negative aspects of value added scores and how they are calculated.

Exercise 8.5

Which other areas of literature could the practitioner have focused on? Do you agree with her choice of focus?

Evaluation (1000 words)

Outline the starting point for your development with the chosen focus:

> The starting point for the evaluation in this instance was whether the DiDA course was enabling the ICT department to add value to the students 'contextual value added' attainment and whether it

would engage and motivate them. It also focused on whether the achievement rates contributed to school improvement targets.

Outline how you have developed classroom practices relating to the chosen focus:

> After a few weeks assimilating ICT skills the students were introduced to the DiDA syllabus using worksheets developed by the writer with the aid of two DiDA text books.

Outline any critical incidents leading to the development of practice:

> A critical incident referred to was the school deciding to switch to Level 1 qualification in May and finding out from the Edexcel website that they had to start the project from the beginning which was unpopular with students and lost two months work. Eventually they were allowed to use a truncated assessment grid to mark Level 2 work where students were failing to perform at this level.

Outline how the classroom strategies you have employed have led to the development of your understanding and professional conduct relating to the chosen issue:

> The students have been encouraged to word independently and take responsibility for their own work. This works well with interested and motivated students but those less able, or motivated, require further tasks and support to keep them on track for completing within the timeframe.

Exercise 8.6

Do you think the evaluation strategies were appropriate?
    What other methods of evaluation of the DiDA course could the practitioner have used with the portfolio?

Conclusion (500 words)

Discuss and critically reflect on what has been learned during the process of producing the portfolio.

> The evaluation has highlighted the importance of students doing at least 8 GCSEs because any fewer would have a negative impact on a

school's VA rating. Schools may also be stricter about GCSE options so that pupils only take subjects in which they can achieve good results.

Explain how this will lead to future professional action and further study:

> After a thorough evaluation of the DiDA course, the school was able to provide evidence that the BTEC First Certificate was the most appropriate ICT course to suit the needs of the learners for delivery during the next academic year. However, the BTEC is only available at level 2, and DiDA is the only ICT qualification at level 1, therefore, it will still be available for some students. What has been learnt from the evaluation will enable the process to be improved.

Extended project

List other areas of future professional action the practitioner could have chosen to investigate. List the areas of future professional action you might choose to investigate. Sort them into order of priority and then consider why you have put them in that order.

Conclusion

At the commencement of this chapter it was stated that a portfolio 'is a popular form of assessment at M Level, probably because it is a move away from the traditional 5000–6000 word essay'. Perhaps on reading and reflecting on this chapter you will realize that it is perhaps not the easy option that it might appear to be at first. It requires good organizational skills to collate the materials and present them in a professional format; it requires good time management skills to organize the timing of the evaluation of the materials and any related follow-ups; it requires clear identification of issues and problems together with appropriate evaluation methodology; it requires reflection on the application of conceptual ideas and theory to professional practice; it requires the critical evaluation of theory/research in the context of professional practice.

To sum up, a portfolio is not an easy option; however, it does provide an interesting and valuable way to evaluate new initiatives within a theoretical framework. It provides evidence of a substantial range of skills and critical reflection which will contribute to the enhancement of your practice.

References

Bell, J. (2005) *Doing Your Research Project*, 4th edn. Maidenhead: Open University Press.

Brown, A. and Dowling, P. (1998) *Doing Research/Reading Research: A Mode of Interrogation for Education*. London: The Falmer Press.

Chetcuti, D., Murphy, P. and Grima, G. (2006) The formative and summative uses of a Professional Development Portfolio: a Maltese case study, *Assessment in Education*, 13(1): 97–112.

Davies, G.R. (2007) *Has the Introduction of DiDA as a Discrete Subject to All Year 10 Students Contributed to School X's Contextual Value Added Figure?* The University of Huddersfield, 30 M Level Credit Assessment.

Klenowkski, V. (2000) Portfolios: promoting teaching, *Assessment in Education*, 7(2): 215–36.

Knight, P.T. (2002) *Small-Scale Research*. London: Sage.

McNiff, J. and Whitehead, J. (2006) *All You Need to Know about Action Research*. London: Sage.

Oxtoby, R. (1979) Problems facing heads of department, *Journal of Further and Higher Education*, 3(1): 46–59.

Simon, M. and Forgette-Giroux, R. (2000) Impact of a content selection framework on portfolio assessment at the classroom level, *Assessment in Education*, 7(1): 83–101.

Tripp, D. (1993) *Critical Incidents in Teaching*. London: Routledge.

Tummons, J. (2005) *Assessing Learning in Further Education*. Exeter: Learning Matters Ltd.

9 Creative approaches to assessment

Observe everything. Communicate well. Draw, draw, draw.

(Frank Thomas, Disney animator,
when asked to give advice to young animators)

Introduction

This chapter explores some of the more creative approaches to M Level assessment. You may find yourself with the opportunity of tackling Masters Level work in a number of different ways. Many courses in education are now introducing more innovative kinds of assessment than the traditional Masters Level written assignment or dissertation that often asks participants to write up a small piece of classroom research. We have included and referred to two examples of alternative assignment tasks. Our *curriculum package* case study involves the development and teaching of a unit of work; the *evidence-based practice* Case study is a critical reflection on a portfolio of evidence. In this chapter we will explore other types of assignment tasks that may be called for at M Level. We will consider different approaches to the presentation of a classroom study, a poster presentation and delivering a seminar paper. We will then consider how you might answer questions about your study in a discussion after a presentation and how you might approach an oral assessment.

The poster presentation

A poster presentation is essentially a visual way of presenting your findings arising from a classroom-based study or investigation which will help you to engage others in a conversation about your work. There is usually an 'opportunity for direct discussion or an exchange of ideas with the presenter' (Akister et al. 2000: 229). This may take the form of a formal oral presentation which may be part of the assessment, opportunities for questions and answers, peer group discussions or of a less formal one-to-one discussion as you talk through the poster with the assessor. Sometimes the assessment process is supported by the submission of a portfolio of evidence which has been generated during the development of the poster. In this case, evidence could include results of literature searches such as copies of relevant articles and précis notes, observational evidence and research data, notes from discussions with participants in the research; lesson plans and evaluations, and any other evidence which is appropriate to the theme of the presentation. National and international conferences often provide space for poster sessions, aimed at those participants who may not yet be ready to give a full paper. You should attend one of these if you get the opportunity, in order to see the many and varied forms in which posters can be presented.

Developing the poster sharpens your ability to select material appropriately, to think critically and to synthesize theory and practice (Bracher et al. 1998). On the poster itself, text is kept to a minimum as the point is to make a strong visual impact as it summarizes and provides information about your study. Visual impact can be created with graphs, bar charts, pie charts, photographs and even clipart to attract attention. You have an opportunity to be as creative as you like here, but the emphasis should be on the clarity with which the design illustrates your message to the reader.

Layout

As a poster, all the elements should be visible from a metre away, so that people can stand and read it comfortably. Keep text at 24pt and headings at 36pt. It is usually better to present the information in columns rather than from left to right, so that in a crowded room readers don't have to fight to get to the beginning of the poster once they have finished reading the first horizontal line. The poster will look more appealing if it is symmetrical in terms of text and images on either a horizontal, vertical or diagonal axis. In terms of colour, a light coloured background with dark text is much easier to read than light text on dark backgrounds. The poster will be less visually chaotic if only two or three colours are used rather than a spectrum.

It is appropriate to provide organizational cues such as a numbering system to guide the reader through the different elements of the poster and you can use white space and the usual reading gravity (left to right, top to bottom) to help you to organize the information so that the poster is read in the appropriate order. Carefully worded headings can also help by summarizing your work, enabling the reader to gain a sense of your study just from reading these alone. Use one font throughout the poster.

Content

The content of the poster should fall into sections which may be linked to the sections in a more traditional written assignment such as those described throughout this book. It is important that you remember that the poster is just a different way of displaying the culmination of your work, not a way to avoid carrying out the detailed analysis, synthesis and evaluation necessary at this level.

The title of a poster will draw people to it and so it deserves careful consideration. One approach might be to think carefully about the message you are trying to convey to the reader and make the strongest claim that you can support with research evidence. An example that could be used for Case study A might be: 'Prior attainment at KS2 affects achievement in ICT at KS3'. The aim of this study was to determine factors which could potentially contribute to underachievement in ICT at KS3. This might be an appropriate title because prior attainment at KS2 was found to be the overriding factor based on the data for which it was possible to develop intervention strategies and the writer makes recommendations based on this claim.

However, this type of title is perhaps more suitable for a poster that is based on a scientific enquiry; in education, it is often difficult to make such bold claims. A title that conveys the purpose and context of the study is equally appropriate. For example: 'An exploratory study into the factors which contribute to pupils not achieving in line with national expectations at KS3 in ICT in one local authority'. The heading should also include your name or, if working in a group, all the people contributing to the study as well as your affiliation, for example, your university and course.

The first section of the poster should outline the context of the study and the rationale; it should also identify the main aims and objectives. The context statement should be brief but enable the reader to understand the confines and parameters of the study. The aims of the research should be elucidated and this section should make clear statements about why the study is important. You should refer to literature which has been key to the research and state how your study adds to current debate. Remember though that text should be kept to the minimum so only the most important theoretical underpinning should be referred to here.

The next part should outline the methodology of your investigation, what you did and how you did it. Explain clearly your chosen methods of data collection such as observations, questionnaires, interviews, focus groups, lesson evaluations, attainment data, etc., and the sequence of activities used in the study. Details of the sample, for example, the number of respondents, the method by which they have been chosen and how they represent 'the total' population might also be appropriate here.

The results section should outline the findings of your study. It is probably helpful to imagine you are writing the first part of the Conclusion section of an assignment here (see Chapter 7). What are the key findings in relation to the aims of the study? This can be done through bullet points but you can also use this as an opportunity to include some diagrams or illustrations. For example, our dissertation Case study includes a number of graphs in the analysis section which would serve to demonstrate the findings with clarity in a poster. See the bar charts showing ICT levels against free school meals and the ICT KS3 levels against KS2 average point scores.

The Conclusion section should outline your recommendations arising from the study. For example, the main recommendations in our dissertation Case study could be outlined as:

• More teaching to improve pupil capability in ICT during KS2.
• More ICT consultant support should be targeted at primary level.
• Intervention strategies should be used to support pupils early in KS3 who have been identified as low achievers at KS2.

This section should outline why the research is significant and go some way to answering the 'So what?' question (see Chapter 7). How the study contributes to understanding and the impact the study has on practice are also important concepts to consider here.

Exercise 9.1

Summarize in no more than 100 words for each section the rationale and the aims of the study, the methodology, the findings and the recommendations that arise from your investigation. This task will help you to decide on the most important points that you need to get across to your audience. You will need to limit the wordage even further when you are refining what will actually appear in your poster.

Creating visual impact

These are appropriate suggestions for slide presentations as well as poster presentations. The most common package for these is Microsoft PowerPoint. There are, however, other sophisticated packages that can be used, most notably Apple's 'Keynote' software.

Try to be creative with bullet points. Changing the usual black bullet icon to an appropriate symbol could add impact to what you are saying. For example, change it to a currency sign when you are making points about resource implications, use an arrow to indicate a recommendation or you might try

      ☺ a smiley face for positive outcomes

      ☻ a sad face for negative ones.

Percentages can be more eye-catching when presented as a pie chart. The use of colour is useful here to separate the different wedges, but remember that you will need to use patterns if you are going to photocopy in black or white. Think carefully about where you put the titles for the different sections, a simple key might be the answer, but this needs to be clearly visible and quickly interpreted, particularly in a poster. Keep the wedges to a maximum of about five or six; you could experiment with using a floating wedge to draw particular attention to one section of the chart.

Quick interpretation should be the mantra when creating any sort of graphic display of numerical data. Many readers switch off if a graph isn't clear almost straight away. Eliminate as much visual distraction such as grid lines, background colour and labelling as possible. Use colour and/or different line types and shading to distinguish between different elements on the graph and limit the amount of data you show in one chart, for example, no more than four lines on a line graph or 6–7 bars on a bar chart. In a histogram, always arrange the bars in order of magnitude, so that the bars show a gradual increase or decrease, rather than giving the impression of jumping around.

Presentation

During the presentation, the poster should be used as a visual aid to outline the context and the aims of the research, the methodology, the findings and the recommendations. You should be able to answer detailed questions about the methodology, about other research in the field and how your study adds to the body of knowledge about your chosen area. You will have much more detail about your study than you can show on your poster and how much of this you can share in an oral presentation depends on the nature of this part of the assessment. One of the most important areas that you might expand on is the theoretical underpinning that would normally be placed in a literature review. This will serve to show your ability to synthesize theory and practice. Assessors will be looking for evidence of critical thinking, ability to develop a coherent argument and contribution to existing knowledge in the field of study. You will find it helpful to prepare a handout, perhaps an A4 version of your poster or one that enables you to add more detail to the content of your poster.

Key points

- The poster is a way of visually presenting your classroom-based study.
- It should succinctly outline the context of your study, the aims and objectives, the methods used to collect data, the findings and recommendations that arise from your research.
- Consideration of the impact of the study is the most important aspect, how the study contributes to understanding and the impact the study has on practice are key to success.
- Visual impact is fundamental; the poster should use as little text as possible and utilize illustrations and diagrams wherever possible.
- The poster is used as a visual aid to oral presentation, where more detail about the nature of the study and the theoretical underpinning supporting your arguments can be given.

Seminar papers

Traditionally a seminar paper is given at a conference and consists of a written paper that can be published as part of the conference report or papers and a presentation to a fairly small group of delegates. As part of a course, you may or may not need to hand in a written paper; the approach might be the submission of a portfolio of supporting material. The time allowed for you to present will be strictly controlled and may include questions or group discussion afterwards. It is paramount that you understand the course guidance regarding the specific requirements of your assessment.

Remember that as a student of education, you will have been in classrooms and witnessed many 'oral presentations'; as a teacher or teacher training student, you will have 'presented' in front of a class. Therefore, presenting your work orally may well be less daunting than for students of many other disciplines. You should have a good understanding of how to explain material in an interesting way. Think about all the things you know about teaching children. How can you make your explanations more compelling? How can you engage your audience rather than expect them to listen passively? In reality, speaking to a peer group is much more daunting than speaking to children. The power relationship is different and you may be uncomfortable about the prospect of talking to a group about a topic about which they are also knowledgeable. Also the assessment aspect is a factor that adds to the tension. Preparation is everything so rehearsal is essential. You need to have planned what you will say and how you will say it, practised the delivery, timed yourself speaking and thought of answers to questions you may be asked.

Remember that the way that you deliver the seminar is going to be assessed as well as the content. Assessors will be looking for a good structure, successful time management, audience engagement, skilful use of audio and visual resources, audibility and clarity, varied intonation, effective use of pauses and silences and a sense of enthusiasm and personal interest.

Content

The basic elements of the presentation will probably include sections similar to those in a written assignment and those described above for a poster. You will need to outline for your audience the problem or issue chosen, the context, the aims of the study, appropriate literature that underpins the debate, methodology, findings, conclusions and your recommendations. Assessors will be looking for a balance between description and analysis, evidence of critical thinking and understanding, coherent arguments supported by relevant and interesting examples, understanding of relevant literature, synthesis between theory and practice and an awareness of the limitations, scope and contribution of the study to existing knowledge.

The principles of teacher exposition (Wragg and Brown 2001; Brown and Hatton 2002) can be used to help you to develop a compelling oral presentation. The opening needs to grab the audience's attention. You may be able to start with an initial stimulus that sets that audience thinking; you might pose a question or ask them to think about their own experiences of a situation. Wragg and Brown (2001) refer to these as a 'tease' or a 'hook'.

It's important then to emphasize the central message. There are a number of reasons for this; first, there is always the possibility, probably a strong one that you will run out of time towards the end of your presentation. If you leave the key information that you want your listeners to take away with them until the end, you might never get there and the presentation is left with no real substance. Second, it is a way of signposting to the audience what is really significant about your work and why your chosen topic is so important.

You will need to identify several key features that will help your audience to understand your work. These could be a central principle, a generalization, examples or an analogy. These are spaced throughout your presentation in a logical sequence that builds understanding gradually. Examples can be drawn from your data and might include:

- illustrations such as graphs and charts that show the trends about which you are talking;
- quotations from participants in the study drawn from interview or questionnaire data;
- descriptions of events that have occurred during classroom observations or teaching;
- evidence from pupils' work

basically, anything that brings your discussion to life.

Throughout your presentation, use signposts to emphasize important points. Phrases like 'In summary ...', 'What is really important to understand is that ...', provide structure to your presentation and signal the most important aspects of your study. It's worth remembering that humour helps to keep attention and make things easier to remember, used appropriately it can help to distil tension and make your presentation more enjoyable for all concerned.

Another consideration is what props you will need to illustrate your explanation. You may have pupils' work or other resources to help you to explain certain aspects of your presentation. Seminar presentations tend to use slide presentations now more than anything else, but using these badly can make your presentation tedious.

Exercise 9.2

Answer the following questions to help you to start to organize your seminar presentation:

- What is your central message?
- What will be the initial stimulus material to open the presentation?
- What examples can you use from your study to illustrate the main points?
- How will you signpost the most important features?
- What props could you use?
- Can you inject some humour into the proceedings?
- How can you engage the audience throughout?

Slide presentations

If you are not an expert, find out from someone who is what the presentation software will actually do. Whilst you don't want all the 'bells and whistles' of animated text and multiple slide-change techniques, you do want to create the maximum visual stimulus. Remember that slide presentation software can be used to show photographs, play music clips or show short films (a video of part of a performance in our curriculum package Case study, for example, could show exactly what children have learned). A remote control is an absolute must to give you the freedom to change slides without having to fumble for a computer keyboard or mouse. You should also take the time to check that your presentation will play on the machines provided in the venue. Different versions of software are not always compatible and a sounder strategy is often to take your own laptop, through which the presentation can be played.

Here are some simple guidelines for making slide presentations that will help you to use this tool effectively during your seminar presentation.

The most important rule is to limit the number of slides and the amount of information on them. Use images, graphs and charts rather than displaying text to illustrate the points that you are making whenever possible. Avoid writing paragraphs, use important words instead. This will help you to avoid the cardinal sin of reading from the slides – they should act as prompts and visual hints rather than as an autocue. The font should be no less than 24pt for readability, if you find yourself apologizing because a screen is too difficult to read, than it's best to avoid using it. If the information is vital, give it on a handout instead. Sanserif fonts are much easier to read than serifs on a screen from a distance. Sentences that use all uppercase letters are also more difficult to read than those in lowercase with appropriate use of capital letters. It is also best to limit punctuation on slides, for example, there is no need to put full stops with bullet points.

Use contrasting colours to make your presentation visually stimulating. Aim for consistency of approach as too many colours can be distracting. Using a design template can help you to achieve consistency, but choose the background carefully. Use a contrasting colour to emphasize a particular word rather than an underline, as underlining often denotes a hyperlink. Learn how to insert internal links as these help you to manage and present information. For example, in a presentation of our action research case study, the writer might speak about the use of pictures in the PECS approach, 'click through' to an example picture, and then 'click back' to the original slide. External hyperlinks can also be useful, providing the place where you are carrying out the presentation has internet access.

Avoid using sounds and flashy transitions as these can be very distracting; pinwheels, content flying in from all directions and text that takes an age to dissolve in can distract from your message and be really frustrating to someone who is trying to take notes as you speak. Artwork should be consistent in style throughout the presentation and used sparingly. All these

advantages to our society' and that 'ICT is playing an increasingly large role in all areas of life – the home, the workplace and leisure pursuits – so children need to be prepared to accept the challenge of a rapidly developing and changing technological world' (BECTA 2000). Through ICT lessons in schools aim to equip pupils with the skills and capability they need for the future while recognizing that the future of ICT is unknown and developments in hardware and software are a constant challenge for schools to adapt to in a changing world.

Rationale

This study aims to explore the factors which influence the levels achieved by pupils in KS3, particularly in ICT, but also in the other core subjects of English, Maths and Science. This could then inform the development of strategies to counteract the factors and increase the number of pupils reaching national expectations, leading to an improvement in pupils' life chances in future cohorts in the LA. Without exploring the reasons for the low levels in the authority it is not possible to make the massive gains required to bring the LA in line with current national levels or expectations.

Context

The three main areas for consideration in this section are: the government school improvement agenda delivered through the national strategy, the role of the researcher in relation to this study and the characteristics of the local authority in which the study is undertaken.

The national strategy

In order to raise standards in secondary schools the DfES on behalf of the government piloted a new national strategy for core subjects in September 2000, this included English, Mathematics, Science and ICT. After a successful pilot year the national programme was unveiled in September 2001 for English and Mathematics, then soon afterwards Science. The Information and Communication Technology strand was piloted during 2001 and launched in 2002.

Researchers' role

Within the strategy the government recognized the need for high quality teachers to lead the strategies and support schools (DfES 2004a: 3). Therefore, when the strategy was launched, consultants were recruited from schools to work within local authorities. Consultants are match-funded by the national strategy and the LA in which they work. The researcher is in the privileged position of being the Secondary ICT Consultant with the remit to raise standards in ICT by improving teaching and learning across both Key Stage 3 and Key Stage 4 (KS4).

[Details of geographical position and some historical data about the area is recorded, along with details regarding the secondary schools in the authority.]

Summary of Key Literature

[The scrutiny of current literature in this study concentrate on two main areas; what underachievement is and what factors contribute to underachievement.]

The broad purpose of this study was to look at why pupils in the local authority do not perform in line with national average in ICT at Key Stage 3. The aims of the research are set out in chronological order, with each being of equal importance as the next and leading to a position where the researcher will be able to discuss the implications of the research which could have the potential to impact directly on the LA and pupil performance in future years:

- To investigate the factors which have the potential to cause pupils to underperform in secondary schools.
- To identify the factors which could potentially be contributing to the underperformance of pupils in ICT at Key Stage 3 in the local authority.
- To ascertain the factors which could have impacted upon the pupils KS3 ICT teacher assessment level in 2006.

Research questions

The questions the research set out to address for each aim were:

1. To investigate the factors which have the potential to cause pupils to underperform in secondary schools
   - What is underperformance?
   - What factors which contribute to underperformance?

2. To identify the factors which co.
   the underperformance of pupils ir
   authority
   - What are the characteristics
   - Which characteristics could b
     ance of pupils at KS3 in the l
   - What factors do teachers belie
     attainment in KS3 ICT?
   - What factors do pupils believe a.
     attainment in KS3 ICT?

3. To ascertain the factors which have impacted upon the pupils KS3
   ICT teacher assessment level in 2006
   - Does the ACORN category of a pupil's home impact on
     their attainment at KS3 in Information and Communica-
     tion Technology?
   - Does being entitled to free school meals have an impact
     on a pupil's attainment at KS3 in ICT?
   - Does the prior attainment of a pupil in the LA impact on
     their attainment at KS3 in ICT?
   - Does the ethnicity of a pupil in the LA impact on their
     attainment in KS3 ICT?
   - Does the number of teachers and the non-specialist teach-
     ers a pupil is taught by in Key Stage 3 impact on their
     attainment in ICT?

Summary

[The chapter is summarized here.]

Chapter 2

Review of the literature

[A comprehensive review of underachievement literature is made, divided into definitions of underachievement and factors that contribute to underachievement. The writer cites a wide range of authorities, including Plewis (1991), Sammons et al. (1994), Weiner et al. (1997), Browne and Mitsos (1998), Broadfoot (1999), Gorard (2000), Kutnick (2000), Demie (2001), Tansel (2002), Bell (2003), Tymms (2003), Smith (2003), Jones and Myhill (2004), Gorard and Smith (2004).]

Community characteristics

[A comprehensive review of literature pertaining to community, and how certain characteristics impact on student attainment, is included. References include Dolton et al. (1999), Rahman et al. (2001), Johnson (2002), Cooper et al. (2003), Smith (2003), Blair (2004), Van de Grift and Houtveen (2006).]

Ethnicity

[A comprehensive review of literature pertaining to ethnicity is included, citing Rampton (1981), Swann (1985), Demie et al. (1997), Kendall (1995, 1998), Demie (2001).]

The teacher's role

[A comprehensive review of literature pertaining to the teacher's role is included citing Wright et al. (1997), Feinstein and Symons (1999), and a number of Ofsted reports.]

The role of adults in the home

[A comprehensive review of literature pertaining to the role of adults is included, citing Douglas (1964), Plowden (1967), Hanushek (1986), Haverman and Wolfe (1995), Coleman et al. (1996), Robertson and Symons (2003), Cooper et al. (2003).]

Prior attainment at Key Stage 2

[A comprehensive review of literature pertaining to prior attainment includes Gorard (2000), Gorard and Smith (2004), Schagen (2006).]

Summary

Disparity in attainment at Key Stage 3 is real and many writers provide documentary evidence to back up their claims that it is linked to their particular area of study. Through all the reading undertaken it does appear that a number of distinguished writers consistently return to three key factors, that of a pupil's socio-economic background, their ethnicity and their prior attainment. As a result, these factors have been explored in detail within the literature review and will be the focus of attention for the research aspect of this study.

Chapter 3

Methodology

In undertaking this study a number of research methods were adopted. This methodology will explain in detail the approach taken and justify the strategies used during the research process.

[Here aims and their link to the chosen methodology are explained.]

Action research

Kemmus and McTaggart (1988: 5) define action research as 'a form of collective self-reflective inquiry undertaken by participants in social situations in order to improve the rationality and justice of their own social or educational practices'. This definition encompasses all the ideals of action research in that it aims to impact upon the person undertaking it through focusing on an issue which is important to them in their role. As the term suggests, action research links practice and research. It is often the case that teachers are very reflective practitioners but by undertaking action research it allows a more in-depth study of practice. Zuber-Skermtt (1996: 85) informs us that action research is a 'critical collaborative inquiry by reflective practitioners being accountable and making results of their practice public'.

Action research was appropriate in this study as it allowed the researcher to gain information and analyse it in a way that no other type of study could. It also provided the vehicle to investigate a key issue for the LA in a systematic and methodical manner. By undertaking action research it was possible to make use of pupil voice to gain a real insight into the pupils' experience of ICT lessons and their family background to help understand issues for pupils as well as providing a mechanism for collecting the perception of teachers regarding underachievement. It also legitimized spending significant time on an in-depth analysis of pupil data and combining information from a number of separate data sets.

The intention was that the results of this study would be made available to teachers within the LA and hopefully foster dialogue between interested parties to influence change. In the words of McNiff (2002), 'If you can improve what you are doing (at least improve your understanding of what you are doing), there is a good chance you will influence the situation you are working in.'

Research methods

For this study there were two separate types of research methods required. The first research involved manipulating secondary documentary evidence in the form of attainment data and information already held in the LA. The second research methods involved collecting primary data from the pupils and teachers.

Research schedule

The relatively short space of time to undertake this study meant that the research schedule was tight. [A table outlining the schedule is included.]

Pilot study

Piloting the research methods has several functions including improving the likelihood that the data collected will be reliable, valid and collect the information expected (Cohen et al. 2000), therefore each research method was piloted.

The initial questionnaire was shared with colleagues before being created, using the online survey. It was then trialled by the researcher and a critical friend to ensure that it worked correctly and provided the expected responses. Following this, the researcher went into one school and observed fourteen mixed ability, gender and ethnic pupils completing the question-naire to ensure that it was suitable for the purpose. This was a useful pilot as it involved pupils who had the same characteristics as the intended respond-ents for the questionnaire and provided feedback to enable the researcher to further explain the required responses for some of the questions before making it available to all pupils.

The interview schedule was again shared with colleagues and improved before being trialled on a teacher who was not employed in a school which was part of the sample. This was deemed as appropriate as the teacher was the same audience as the intended respondents and could provide feedback before the interviews were conducted for real. It also confirmed that the interview questions provided the stimulus for the expected discussions regarding underachievement.

Sample

[The sample size and characteristics of the sample are here discussed in detail, and literature is used to support the choice of sample and questions of ethics.]

Multiple methods and triangulation

Hendricks (2006) argues that triangulation helps increase the credibility and impacts on the validity of the study. Miles and Huberman (1994) and Hammersley and Atkinson (1995) concur that triangulation is a way of double-checking data and supporting its validity through collecting information from elsewhere.

In this study, triangulation took place by collecting information from documentary evidence, questionnaires and through semi-structured interviews. This is advocated by Cohen, Manion and Morrison (2000: 12) who see triangulation as 'the use of two or more methods of data collection in the study'. The study also used both qualitative and quantitative data collection methods. In addition, observations outside the remit of this study and the views of colleagues, teachers and pupils in the local authority were used to triangulate findings.

Conduct of research

In order to complete the study the following steps were taken:

Step 1 Contacted schools to gain permission to use pupil data, interview teachers and ask some pupils to complete questionnaire.

Step 2 Collated local authority data into Microsoft Excel and produced graphs and pivot charts to ascertain whether there was a relationship between attainment in KS3 ICT and factors such as ACORN classification, prior attainment, ethnicity and FSM.

Step 3 Produced, discussed with critical friends then piloted questionnaire and semi-structured interview schedule and issued questionnaire to pupils for completion as an online survey.

Step 4 Imported questionnaire data in Microsoft Excel, performed calculations and produced graphs to demonstrate relationships between pupil's attainment in ICT and a pupil's family background, their parents' education and the parental involvement in the pupil's education as well as the impact of non-specialist teachers and a consistent teacher within an academic year.

Step 5 Undertook teacher interviews.

Step 6 Transcribed and reviewed teacher interviews with a focus on teachers' expectations of pupil attainment and what they perceived could raise standards in ICT at Key Stage 3.

Step 7 Assimilated information from LA data, questionnaire and teacher interviews to ensure triangulation and produce conclusions.

Limitations of the research

[Caveats regarding the limitations are discussed, including size of sample, along with benefits of, for example, using online questionnaires and making transcripts of interviews.]

Chapter 4

Analysis and discussion

This chapter attempts to discuss the main findings from the study and link it to the work of other writers. It is intended to present the data and observations in a succinct manner before looking at the implications in the final chapter.

[Graphs and tables are presented and discussed.]

Community characteristics findings

The community characteristic findings come from the LA data and provide a clear indication of the issues facing schools and the local authority as a whole.

ACORN classification

Figure 4.1 shows that there is a difference between the average level achieved in KS3 ICT by a child classified as living in a hard-pressed area when compared with a child classified as living in a wealthy achiever area. This supports the view of Smith (2003: 581) who states that 'pupils from relatively more economically disadvantaged homes were less successful in school', although the difference in ICT is only slight.

Analysed together, this statistical evidence does indicate that the background of the child does impact upon the level they achieve at the end of Key Stage 3. In subjects which are tested, there is a greater difference with Mathematics showing the most significant difference between pupils from deprived backgrounds and those from relatively well off communities. This supports the findings of similar studies such as Cooper et al. (2003) who found that social deprivation is a key factor in educational underachievement.

Free school meals

Figure 4.3 shows the average level achieved in ICT for pupils who are entitled to free school meals against those who do not qualify. It shows that there is a

References

Baker, M. (1998) Poverty gap beats gender divide. 16 January 1998 Available at: www.tes.co.uk [accessed 14 November 2006].

Baker, S., Bird, M., Carty, J., Faulkner, D., Gomm, R., Hammersley, M., Mercer, M, Perrott, M., Swann, J. and Woods, P. (2003) *Research Methods in Education.* Milton Keynes: The Open University Press.

BECTA (2000) *Parents and ICT.* Available at: www.becta.org.uk [accessed 3 April 2007].

Bell, D. (2003) Access and achievement in urban education: 10 years on, a speech to the Fabian Society, Thursday, November 20 2003. Available at: www.guardian.co.uk [accessed 20 November 2007].

Blair, T. (2004) Foreword, in *Breaking the Cycle: Taking Stock of Progress and Priorities for the Future.* London: ODPM.

Broadfoot, P. (1999) Assessment and the emergence of modern society, in B. Moon and P. Murphy (eds) *Curriculum in Context.* Milton Keynes: Open University Press.

Brown and Dowling (2001) *Doing Research/Reading Research: A Mode of Interrogation for Education.* London: Falmer Press.

Browne, K. and Mitsos, E. (1998) Gender differences in education: the underachievement of boys. *Sociology Review,* cited in J. Burns and P. Bracey, Boys' underachievement: issues, challenges and possible ways forward, *Westminster Studies in Education,* 24(2).

Burton, D. and Bartlett, S. (2005) *Practitioner Research for Teachers.* London: Paul Chapman.

CACI (2006) *The ACORN User Guide.* London: CACI. Available at: www.caci.co.uk [accessed 26 March 2007].

Cohen, L., Manion, L. and Morrison, K. (2000) *Research Methods in Education.* London: RoutledgeFalmer.

Coleman, J. et al. (1996) *Equality of Educational Opportunity.* Washington, DC: US GPO.

Cooper, M., Lloyd-Reason, L. and Wall, S. (2003) Social deprivation and educational underachievement: lessons from London, *Education and Training,* 45(2).

Demie, F. (2001) Ethnic and gender differences in educational achievement and implications for school improvement strategies. *Educational Research,* 43(1).

Demie, F., Reid, F., Reid, A. and Butler, R. (1997) *Pupil Achievement and Ethnic Background: Results of the Analysis of the 1997 National Curriculum.* London: Southwark Education.

Denscombe, M. (1998) *The Good Research Guide.* Buckingham: Open University Press.

DfES (2002) *Key Stage 3 National Strategy: Key Messages from the ICT Launch.* London: DfES.

DfES (2003) *Primary School (Key Stage 2) Performance Tables.* Available at: http://www.dfes.gov.uk [accessed 3 April 2007].

DfES (2004a) *Key Stage 3 National Strategy: A Handbook for Consultants.* London: DfES.

DfES (2004b) *An Introduction to the Key Stage 3 Strategy for Year 7 Parents and Carers.* London: DfES.

DfES (2006a) *Secondary School (KS3) Achievement and Attainment Tables 2006.* Available at: http://www.dfes.gov.uk [accessed 3 April 2007].

DfES (2006b) *Making Good Progress.* London: DfES.

Dolton, P., Makepeace, G., Hotton, S. and Audas, R. (1999) *Making the Grade: Education, the Labour Market and Young People.* York: Joseph Rowntree Organisation.

Douglas, J. (1964) *The Home and the School.* London: MacGibbon and Kee.

Feinstein, L. and Symons, J. (1999) Attainment in secondary school. *Oxford Economic Papers 51.*

Fischer Family Trust (2005a) *Fischer Education Project 2005: Methodology Input Measures.* Available at: www.fischertrust.org [accessed 4 April 2007].

Fischer Family Trust (2005b) *Fischer Education Project 2005: Guidance – Using Estimates Effectively.* Available at: www.fischertrust.org [accessed 4 April 2007].

Gorard, S. (2000) 'Underachievement' is still an ugly word: reconsidering the relative effectiveness of schools in England and Wales, *Journal of Education Policy*, 15(5).

Gorard, S. and Smith, E. (2004) What is 'underachievement' at school? *School Leadership and Management*, 24(2).

Hanushek, E. (1986) The economics of schooling: production and efficiency in public schools, *Journal of Economic Literature*, 24.

Hanushek, E. (1992) The trade-off between child quantity and quality, *Journal of Political Economy*, 100(1).

Haverman, R. and Wolfe, B. (1995) The determinants of children's attainment: a review of methods and findings, *Journal of Economic Literature*, 33.

Hendricks, C. (2006) *Improving Schools through Action Research: A Comprehensive Guide for Educators*. Boston: Pearson Education.

Higgs, G., Bellin, W., Farrell, S. and White, S. (1996) Educational attainment and social disadvantage: contextualizing school league tables, *Regional Studies*, 31(8).

Johnson, M. (2002) 'Choice' has failed the poor, *The Times Educational Supplement*, 22 November.

Jones, S. and Myhill, D. (2004) Seeing things differently: teachers' construction of underachievement, *Gender and Education*, 16(4).

Kemmus and McTaggart (1988) cited in L. Cohen, L. Manion, and K. Morrison (2000) *Research Methods in Education*. London: RoutledgeFalmer.

Kendall, L. (1995) *Report on the Analysis of 1994 Examination Results: NFER/AMA Project on Examination Results in Context*. London: Association of Metropolitan Authorities.

Kendall, L. (1998) *Report on the Analysis of 1997 Examination Results: NFER/AMA Project on Examination Results in Context*. London: Association of Metropolitan Authorities.

Kutnick, P. (2000) Girls, boys and school achievement, *International Journal of Educational Development*, 20(1).

LSC (2006) *Key Learning and Skills Facts: Yorkshire and the Humber, 2006/07*. Available at: www.lsc.gov.uk [accessed 1 April 2007].

McNiff, J. (2002) *Action Research for Professional Development: Concise Advice for New Action Researchers*. Available at: www.jeanmcniff.com [accessed 27 July 2005].

Miles and Huberman (1994) cited in D. Burton and S. Bartlett (2005) *Practitioner Research for Teachers*. London: Paul Chapman Publishing.

Miliband, D. (2002) Foreword to *Framework for Teaching ICT Capability: Year 7, 8 and 9*. London: DfES.

Miliband, D. (2004) Personalised learning: building a new relationship with schools. Speech at North of England Education conference, Belfast. Available at: www.dfes.gov.uk [accessed 13 April 2007].

Munn and Drever (1999) *Using Questionnaires in Small-Scale Research: A Teachers Guide.* Edinburgh: SCRE Publications.

Ofsted (1997) *From Failure to Success.* London: HMI.

Ofsted (2004) *Statistical Profile for Education in Schools.* London: HMI.

ONS (2001) *Resident Population: by Ethnic Group, 2001.* London: Office for National Statistics. Available at: http://www.statistics.gov.uk [accessed 7 April 2007].

Oppenheim (1998) cited in L. Cohen, L. Manion and K. Morrison (2000) *Research Methods in Education.* London: RoutledgeFalmer.

Plewis, I. (1991) Underachievement: a case of conceptual confusion, *British Education Research Journal*, 17(4).

Plowden, B. (1967) *The Plowden Report: Children and Their Primary Schools: A Report of the Central Advisory Council of Education.* London: HMSO.

QCA (2004) *ICT 2002/3 Annual Report on Curriculum and Assessment.* London: QCA.

Rahman, M., Palmer, G. and Kenway, P. (2001) *Monitoring Poverty and Social Exclusion.* York: Joseph Rowntree Foundation.

Rainey, D. and Murova, O. (2004) Factors influencing educational achievement, *Applied Economics*, 36.

Rampton (1981) *West Indian Children in Our Schools.* London: HMSO.

Robertson, D. and Symons, J. (2003) Do peer groups matter? Peer group versus schooling effects on academic attainment, *Economica*.

Robinson, P. (1997) *Literacy, Numeracy and Economic Performance: CEP.* London: London School of Economics.

Sammons, P., Thomas, S., Mortimore, P., Owen, C. and Pennell, H. (1994) *Assessing School Effectiveness.* London: International School Effectiveness and Improvement Centre.

Schagen, I. (2006) The use of standardized residuals to derive value-added measures of school performance. *Educational Studies* 12(2).

Smith, E. (2003) Understanding underachievement: an investigation into the differential attainments of secondary school pupils. *British Journal of Sociology of Education*, 24(5).

Stephens, L. (1998) *Schaum's Outline of Statistics: Theory and Problems of Statistics.* Philadelphia: McGraw-Hill.

Swann (1985) *Education for All*. London: HMSO.

Tansel, A. (2002) Determinants of school attainment of boys and girls in Turkey: individual, household and community factors, *Economics of Education Review*, 21.

Thorndike, R. (1963) *The Concepts of Over and Underachievement*. New York: Teachers College Press.

Tymms, P. (2003) Standards over time, presentation at British Educational Research Association (BERA) annual conference, Edinburgh.

Van de Grift, W. and Houtveen, A. (2006) Underperformance in primary schools, *School Effectiveness and School Improvement*, 17(3).

Weiner, G., Arnot, M. and David, M. (1997) Is the future female? Female success, male disadvantage and changing patterns in education, in A.H. Halsey, H. Lauder, P. Brown and A. Wells (eds) *Education: Culture, Economy and Society*. Oxford: Oxford University Press.

Whitehouse, P. (2006) 'Remarkable' employment success story praised by Minister, *The Yorkshire Post*, 22 August.

Woodhead (1998) in C. Dean (1998) Failing boys, 'public burden number one', *Times Educational Supplement*, 27 November.

Wright, S., Horn, S. and Sanders, W. (1997) Teacher and classroom context effects on student achievement: implications for teacher evaluation, *Journal of Personnel Evaluation in Education*.

Zuber-Skeritt, O., (1996) cited in L. Cohen, L. Manion and K. Morrison (2000) *Research Methods in Education*. London: RoutledgeFalmer.

List of Tables

List of Figures

Figure 4.2 Graph showing difference between expected and actual number of pupils if there were no relationship between the ICT level achieved and the ACORN category

Figure 4.3 Graph showing average KS3 ICT level against FSM

Figure 4.4 Graph showing average KS3 ICT level against KS2 APS

Figure 4.5 Bubble graph showing the number of pupils at each ICT level for all the APS's at KS2

Figure 4.6 Graph showing difference between expected and actual number of pupils if there were no relationship between the ICT level achieved and prior attainment

Figure 4.7 Graph showing the perceived number of teachers pupils had teach them in KS3 and the average number of specialist and non-specialist

List of Appendices

Appendix 1 Characteristics of LA schools LA Data Team (2006)

Appendix 2 Data included in the documentary research

Appendix 3 DfES (2003: 3) Primary School (Key Stage 2) Performance Tables

Appendix 4 Copy of online questionnaire

Appendix 5 Copy of interview schedule

Appendix 6 Transcripts of semi-structured interviews

Appendix 7 Characteristics of documentary data sample

Appendix 8 Characteristics of respondents to questionnaire

Appendix 9 Copy of letter sent to head teachers

Appendix 10 Average KS3 result by ACORN Classification

Appendix 11 Average KS3 Result by KS2 APS

Appendix 12 KS3 ICT TA Against Prior APS at KS2

Appendix 13 Highest NVQ or equivalent level held by individuals LSC (2006: 9)

Case study B
Music Curriculum Package
Teaching Strategy

Modelling and explaining Renaissance music in Year 7

Michelle Bentley

Introduction

This assignment was produced whilst on second teaching practice placement at an 11–16 mixed community secondary school.

[School is described in detail and its recent Ofsted report used to underpin description of the music department, the school and its pupils.]

The following curriculum package will be taught to a Year 7 class. The topic, Renaissance Music, is currently taught as part of the department scheme of work. The focus of this package will be on *modelling and explaining* and will demonstrate the benefits that this specific teaching strategy has on teaching and learning. A Year 7 class has been selected for this project as they are relatively new to the school and the previous topic provides a good basis of knowledge for learning about Renaissance music (for an overview of KS3 music, see Appendix 1).

[Further information detailing how the unit fits in terms of progression is given.]

The topic will be assessed in line with the department's assessment policy. [Further details of this are included here.]

The specific class to be taught are [detailed description of class and its range of abilities included.]

The group has been selected not only because of the stage the pupils are at in their schooling but also because of the wide range of abilities noted from their last module assessment grades (in Appendix 2) ranging from NC level 2a to 4b. This will enable me to assess the effectiveness of my modelling and explaining with reference to all levels of ability, as well as facilitate differentiation through outcome and task. Pupils will complete a variety of tasks involving listening, appraising, composing and performing through group, class and pair work, as well as individual study. A homework task will be set to reaffirm class work.

Modelling and especially explaining were shown as areas of weakness during my first placement teaching practice: this opportunity to devise a curriculum package showing awareness and progression of a particular teaching strategy provides an opportunity for me to develop this area of my teaching. The Department for Education and Skills National Strategy (2006) states that varied teaching strategies can 'fire pupils' imagination' which can 'make musical learning more interesting, exciting and effective' (DfES 2006: 7), highlighting the importance of teacher awareness and practice of various teaching strategies.

Literature review

Throughout my background reading in the areas of modelling and explaining it has become apparent that recent research can be split into two broad categories: discussions about the benefit, need and use of these strategies alongside scientific explanations of how and why these particular strategies are successful. For the purpose of this assignment I will be focusing on literature which discusses the practicalities of modelling and explaining, as well as the benefits and implementation in planning for and delivering these strategies in a classroom context.

One of the main issues in teaching in secondary school music lessons today is providing pupils of varying abilities with the knowledge and skills they need to learn in the classroom. Differentiation by task and outcome goes some way to solving this problem, however Joyce et al. (1997) argue that a variety of teaching strategies is what is needed, and this is the only way to include and develop the knowledge of all pupils with varying abilities:

> Whether at the class or school level, the broader the range of teaching approaches and learning experiences arranged for our children, the more likely we are to reach our goal of educating all students.

(Joyce et al. 1997: 25)

LESSON 1

Context
[As this is the first lesson of the unit the context that is described above is outlined here.]

Learning Objectives
By the end of this lesson pupils will: • Understand the dates of the Renaissance period and instruments • Develop listening skills by completing SET 1 questions in the starter listening handbook • Learn about and use the Aeolian scale and compose a short melody using this with a drone accompaniment on keyboards **NC POS** : 1b, c, 2b, 3a, b, c, 4a, b, d, 5a, b, c, e

Assessment Indicators
By the end of the lesson: **All pupils will have:** attempted the listening starter, participated in a class discussion, made notes on Renaissance instruments and dates, composed a short melody using the Aeolian scale. **Most pupils will have:** Completed the listening starter, participated in a class discussion, made notes on Renaissance instruments and dates, composed a short melody using the Aeolian scale and added the drone. **Some more able pupils will have:** Completed the listening starter, participated actively in a class discussion, made detailed notes on Renaissance instruments and dates, composed a melody using the Aeolian scale and added the drone part in time.

Key Skills
[How the lesson contributes to key skills and dimensions is outlined here.]

Differentiation
• Questions have been carefully formulated for the starter activity so that all pupils can answer them. There is scope for more able pupils to develop their answers further. • Pupils will be monitored throughout the composing activity to ensure all are working to their capability – the end of last module test scores from last term will be consulted to establish which pupils are more able and those who struggled with composing previously. • All will be encouraged to participate in discussion.

Equipment/Resources
[Resources used are outlined here.]

LESSON ACTIVITIES

INTRODUCTION
Give out folders and take register (**5 mins**)

Briefly explain this module [detail is outlined here.]

Refer to lesson objectives on AV

Starter Activity (**10 mins**)
First we are going to hear a musical example of Renaissance music.
Read through questions on listening handbook and give examples of possible answers.
Hear musical examples, fill out answers and mark – *explain that these handbooks are not about marks but about developing knowledge – write in any notes that you have not got during discussion of answers.*

Discussion

TIMELINE: 'setting the scene'. (**2 mins**)
Relate to last module: 800–1400 medieval **1400–1600 Renaissance**

INSTRUMENTS (**3 mins**)
Put instrument sheet up on AV and discuss – only do first page of two.
Explain which instruments differ from those in Medieval period – introduction of viols ... questioning *what do you think viols are?*

SCALE (**5 mins**)
We are going to look at a new scale ... Aeolian scale.
Remember the Dorian scale ... what note did it start on? D
Aeolian starts on A! Play the scale on piano, stating that it is all white notes from a-a. Get pupil to come and play scale.

DRONE
Drone – what's a drone? 2 note accompaniment. Teacher and pupil demo – pupil playing drone, teacher playing scale over the top.

Instruction (**10 mins**)
By the end of today I want you all to be able to play a short melody using the Aeolian scale.
In pairs, one at either end of the keyboard, I want you to compose a **2 BAR** melody, starting and ending on the note A using the Aeolian scale.

Model TEACHER'S TUNE on board – *get class to fill in notes using Aeolian scale*

*Draw chart for '**YOUR TUNE**' and copy into books* – **YOU SHOULD HAVE A MELODY EACH!!!**

EXTENSION – if you complete this, get your partner to play the drone while you play your melody, then swap.
Pupil and teacher demo – get pupil to play drone while I play my melody.

REMINDER: Recap on note lengths from previous module – in books on page 2 – remember 4 beats in a bar.   (**3 mins**)
Get pupil to recap task to rest of class – ask class if pupil has missed anything out.

DEVELOPMENT
Time to compose and practise melody. Once in pairs, announce time limit (**10 mins**) and send pupils to practice rooms. Pupil to recap task to class. Teacher reiterate task as pupils leave for practice rooms.

PUPIL WATCH – Keep pupils 15, 20 and 22 in room – teacher tutor has mentioned that they struggle to stay on task in practice rooms.

Differentiate this task by monitoring progress and helping and moving on individual pupils with the support of teacher tutor

CONCLUSION   (**10 mins**)
REGROUP – Hear a few examples from pupils and discuss good points of composition and areas for improvement next lesson. Encourage 'good audience' and clapping after performances. AFL.

Plenary   (**5 mins**)
Talk about what we have learnt today. Recap on drone, Aeolian scale, instruments and timeline.
Pack away and sit down.
Briefly discuss next lesson – question and answer phrases to extend melody, adding drone.   (**2 mins**)

[Six sets of lesson plans, observations, evaluations and all the resources are included.]

Evaluation

The Renaissance unit is placed well in the Year 7 modules of work (see Appendix 1). It follows on from the Medieval module which progresses through listening, composing and performing in the same way. Kerry (1998: 108, 117), as mentioned in the literature part of this package, lays heavy emphasis on the importance of linking new information with prior knowledge and this was done via explanation throughout this module. It proved highly effective as pupils had already progressed through lessons following this listening, composing and performing format and were comfortable with this arrangement.

Looking specifically at explaining and modelling which was the focus of this package, I have many points to evaluate. First, it is important to consider the effectiveness of my modelling and explaining. It became apparent during teaching the first Renaissance lesson that the timings I had predicted for explaining information and tasks had been greatly underestimated. This was noted by the teacher tutor (see Observation) where it was mentioned that pace needed to be thought about in greater detail. During the lesson itself, I followed Petty's advice to 'simplify to the point where you are distorting the truth somewhat' (Petty 2004: 162) by providing shortened explanations of instruments and cutting out the explanation of the drone completely. However, this was with the intention of shortening the explanation to catch up on lost time rather than simplifying detail, and although the learning could still take place, this could have been problematic. For lessons 3 and 4 explanations were condensed and signposts were used so that pupils could gauge the importance of the information they were being given. As Petty (2004) describes, providing a 'hierarchy of importance' shows a good explanation (Petty 2004: 166) and stating that 'This part is important, listen carefully' to the class is advantageous in gaining pupils' attention.

I also found it very effective for pupils to get involved in explanations.

[Further evaluation of the use of this strategy follows.]

Throughout most of my classroom explanations I tried to use as much modelling as possible: teacher and pupil. As discussed in the literature review of this curriculum package, the DfES regard modelling as a high priority teaching strategy and describe it as a 'powerful' method 'that can be used to demonstrate a range of skills and processes' (DfES 2002: 144). During the explanation parts of lessons I modelled the task and information to pupils. For example, in lesson 1 I played the Aeolian scale to pupils on the electric piano. I then asked a pupil to also come and play the scale, and as noted in the lesson evaluation pupils were enthusiastic and many hands went up to offer to come and model. This also helped to keep the explanation lively and memorable. As Mills (2005) discusses, 'teachers who are teaching music musically draw in students' (Mills 2005: 20) and this was enormously apparent in parts of the lessons in which I have used teacher followed by pupil modelling. This conforms to Batho's belief that teaching should commence with 'teacher explication and demonstration to the whole class' (Batho 2002: 80). This design continued throughout every lesson providing format and clarity for pupils.

[A discussion about the benefits of including pupils modelling follows.]

Assessment is the key to progression in the classroom and during this module I have incorporated summative and formative assessment.

[The curriculum package is evaluated further by an extended discussion of the pupils' achievement throughout the unit. Examples of pupils work are discussed.]

Conclusion

It is clear from the above evaluation that there are many successes from teaching this unit of work with a focus on modelling and explaining. The starter listening activities worked well and provided consistency to each lesson. Explanations aided development and teacher modelling helped pupils relate to the task and actually *see* what they were being asked to do, as well as learning *how* to do it. Pupil modelling was used as an extension of this and helped to keep the class engaged; willing and wanting to take part.

As Joyce et al. (1997) state, 'the broader the range of teaching approaches ... the more likely we are to reach our goal of educating all students' (Joyce et al. 1997: 25). Taking this into consideration, the best way to improve this package would be to consciously incorporate as many teaching strategies as possible, providing an amalgamation of approaches to benefit all pupils. To develop the package further it would be beneficial for pupils to actually see the instruments they are composing for, although this was not possible during this unit. Pupils' learning could also be developed by going to a live concert of Renaissance music; through my discussions with pupils during lessons it has become clear that almost all have never been to a live classical instrumental concert, an event that I believe could benefit pupils' musical appraisal, composing and listening skills dramatically. I could have developed this area further in the classroom by playing my instruments (violin and flute) in the Renaissance style and would try and integrate this if teaching the unit again. Further improvement could be gained by the use of ICT in learning. [Some discussion about how ICT could be included in this unit of work follows.]

My teaching has improved considerably throughout this package and this can be seen when looking at the teacher tutor observations. Because I have had to consider my chosen teaching strategy in depth, my planning has been more consistent and I have learnt how to synthesize lessons, developing on pupils assessed knowledge. Specifically my explaining methods have become clearer and more focused and I have observed the benefits of teacher and pupil modelling. I am developing these strategies further now in the other modules that I teach.

Appendices (The following were included.)

- KS3 Schemes of Work at SP2 – Overview
- Year 7 Renaissance class list and assessment grades
- Renaissance starter listening handbook and CD
- Renaissance instruments AV
- Renaissance end of module listening test sheet and answers
- Renaissance end of module listening test NC levels
- Renaissance performance NC levels
- End of Module Self Evaluation Sheet

References

Adams, P. (2001) Planning to teach musically, in C. Philpott (ed.) *Learning to Teach Music in the Secondary School: A Companion to School Experience*. Abingdon: RoutledgeFalmer.

Batho, R. (2002) Teaching literacy across the curriculum, in V. Ellis (ed.) *Learning and Teaching in Secondary Schools*. Exeter: Learning Matters Ltd.

Cohen, L., Manion, L. and Morrison, K. (1996) *A Guide to Teaching Practice*. London: Routledge.

DfES (2002) *Module 6: Modelling, Training Materials for the Foundation Subjects*. London: DfES.

DfES (2004) *Explaining Unit 8, Key Stage 3 National Strategy: Pedagogy and Practice*. London: DfES.

DfES (2006) *Secondary National Strategy: Foundation Subjects: KS3 Music*. London: DfES.

Dix, P. (2007) *Taking Care of Behaviour, Practical Skills for Teachers*. Edinburgh: Pearson Education Ltd.

Joyce, B., Calhoun, C. and Hopkins, D. (1997) *Models of Learning: Tools for Teaching*. Buckingham: Open University Press.

1.2 Rationale

[Government legislation regarding children with Harry's needs is explained. The writer observes that Harry's care has become fragmented and describes the individuals and services that can be used to improve and provide seamless care for Harry.]

1.3 Aims

The practitioner will use a combination of existing knowledge about Harry and published research to define a strategy for working with Harry. The first aim of the research is to explore whether a tailored approach is more effective than no intervention, using interviews and observations with and without the use of an intervention. The practitioner will then examine the effects of the intervention on helping Harry to stay on task, and reducing the number of times Harry shows distress using both interviews and observations. Using the results the practitioner aims to continue to develop the strategy to suit Harry's needs.

2.0 Literature Review

This section will look at the impact of autism on learning and the implications for learning. It will go on to relate this to inclusion. Finally, possible interventions for Harry will be discussed.

2.1 The impact of autism on learning

Kanner (1943) first recommended the existence of autism, where he identified a number of characteristics shared by those people with autism. These included:

- lack of desire to communicate verbally;
- echolalic verbal utterances;
- fear in strange or unexpected situations;
- repetitive behaviours demonstrated.

(taken from Wall 2004: 6)

Since Kanner, there has been an overwhelming amount of research into every aspect of autism.

Baron-Cohen (1995) suggests that people with autism have a lack of *'theory of mind'*, or 'mind-blindness' which means that they cannot recognize the mental states of others. Frith (1989) suggests that those with autism lack *central coherence* which means that they have difficulties in recognizing a whole concept rather than just the details. Most people naturally place information into a context and see the 'bigger picture'. Another model proposes that people with autism have difficulties in *'executive functioning'*. Executive functioning allows us to transfer our attention from one area to another smoothly and use our thoughts to solve problems (Norman and Shallice 1980).

Current government guidance *Autistic Spectrum Disorders: Good Practice Guidelines* (DfES 2002) suggests that children with autism share a 'triad of impairments'. Suggested by Wing (1996), this theory remains consistent with theory of mind, central coherence and executive function models. It defines impairments shared by those with autism as social communication, social interaction and imagination.

There is some overlapping and consistency across the above theories which are all well documented (Baron-Cohen 1995; Lord 1995). The difficulties that they suggest are consistent with those seen in Harry prior to the study and have huge implications for inclusion and access to the Foundation Stage curriculum. Hanbury (2005) suggests the 'rich, fast-flowing stream of communication' (p. 18) in the classroom places the autistic child in a difficult and scary world. Socially, Harry can find it difficult to recognize rules and expectations, and to interpret the feelings of others. A difficulty using imagination means that Harry may find it difficult to talk about absent objects, engage in pretend play and talk about future events.

2.2 Inclusion

[Policies and reports regarding inclusion are discussed, in particular the Warnock Report (DES 1978), the Audit Commission (2002) and the White Paper *Removing Barriers to Achievement* (DfES 2004). The reasons why early years settings are already considered fairly inclusive are given and supported by literature e.g. Nutbrown (1998).]

2.3 Interventions

For anyone to learn and achieve, a number of basic needs have to be met first. Maslow (1943) suggested that before people can operate on a higher level, they must have their physiological and safety needs met. It then follows that before Harry can begin to access the curriculum, he must first feel secure.

[Detailed discussion of intervention programmes follows.]

2.4 The approaches used within this study

[An approach using PECs and TEACCH methods is proposed and explained. PECS is the Picture Exchange Communication System using a child's visual strengths. TEACCH is the Treatment and Education of Autistic and Related Communication Handicapped Children and is a life approach based on the strengths that the person with autism already has. Arguments regarding the possible drawbacks of such an approach are supported by literature e.g. Schreibman (2000); Tutt, Powell and Thornton (2006).]

The main aims of this study are:

- To assess whether a tailored approach is more effective than no intervention.
- To help Harry to stay on task.
- To reduce the number of times Harry becomes distressed.

3.0 Methodology and conduct of the research

This section will begin with a broad overview and justification of the type of research that was used within this study. It will then go on to explain how this study was conducted, choices that were made and why.

3.1 Principles and practice of action research

Brown and Dowling (1998) define action research as 'a term which is applied to projects in which practitioners seek to effect transformations in their own practices'. It is true of any good practitioner that they stand back, question and reflect on their own practice. Action research brings a systematic and disciplined approach to this familiar exercise (Koshy 2005). Definitions of action research by different writers often differ slightly but share common vocabulary, namely 'reflection', 'development' and 'improvement'.

Kurt Lewin (1948) is considered to be one of the founding figures of action research. As part of a controversial group in Germany before the Second World War, Lewin suggested that it was not possible to produce quantitative results based on how subjects behaved in an experimental situation, but that the interaction between experimenter and subject should be part of the object of investigation from the beginning (Danziger 1990). In America, Lewin went on to research social processes and was very much concerned with the cyclic process that we know as part of action research today. The approach involves a series of steps, 'each of which is composed of a circle of planning, action and fact-finding about the result of the action' (Lewin 1946, reproduced in Lewin 1948: 206).

Action research emerged in Britain in the 1970s, one influence being the Humanities Curriculum Project (1967–72) and Lawrence Stenhouse who promoted the idea of 'teacher as researcher' (McNiff 2002). More recently, developments in England and Wales have reflected the recognition and value placed upon action research, such as small research grants made available by the Teacher Training Agency and the DfES (Koshy 2005). Action research is now recognized as a tool for professional learning and professional development (McNiff 2002). In this small-scale research project, the practitioner wanted to improve her own practice through reflection and find a starting point for collaborative enquiry. Convery (1998) suggests that for reflection to truly influence practice, collaborative discussions must take place, as individual reflection tackles immediate rather than underlying problems. The practitioner hoped to further her own professional development and begin a 'reflective dialogue' in the setting by discussing research findings with colleagues.

[The advantages of using action research are discussed in detail.]

3.2 Conduct of the research

[The main aim of the study is reiterated.]

3.2.1 Quantitative/qualitative research

[The relative merits of each are discussed, with reference to literature and linked to Harry's behaviour.]

One limitation of qualitative research and also action research is that because it involves the researcher, findings may be considered a creation of the researcher rather than fact (Denscombe 1998). It is for this reason that researchers often use a combination of qualitative and quantitative approaches (Clough and Nutbrown 2002) in order to triangulate their research findings, see Section 3.2.5.

3.2.2 Research instruments used

Observations were used to gather data for this study. An open observation approach was used, as using a structured observation schedule would impose structure at an early stage and restrict the data collected (Brown and Dowling 1998). A preferred method was to make more general, ethnographic observations so that different interpretations and foci would be possible, incidents could be related and emerging trends explored (Hopkins 1998). The observations were carried out by the researcher herself. Brown and Dowling (1998) caution researchers using this method as they rely on the researcher's interpretation of events. However, as a Foundation Stage teacher where assessment relies on observations, it was considered that the practitioner was sufficiently experienced in observing. This method had the advantage of being flexible as the practitioner worked full-time with the sample child and it would be possible to return to the field after analysis to do further observations. Harry was observed for five days without a specific intervention (Monday to Friday) and for five days with an intervention (Monday to Friday). An example can be seen in Appendix 1.

[The way in which semi-structured and formal interviews with both Harry and his Mum were conducted are here described, with supporting literature, Brown and Dowling (1998); Hopkins (2002).]

3.2.3 Ethics

Whether a small- or large-scale project, it is important as both a researcher and a professional that ethical issues are addressed. Failure to do so would not only compromise research but could also compromise the professional position of a practitioner. Burton and Bartlett (2005) refer to *The Ethical Guidelines for Educational Research* by the British Research Association (BERA 2003) and from these infer that there are five key issues that teacher researchers should be concerned with, namely consent; honesty and openness; access to findings; researcher effects; and anonymity.

Consent was sought from the Headteacher of the centre as well as Harry's parents who received an outline of the nature of the research in writing before they made the decision to consent. Staff within the base room were briefed in a team meeting about both the nature of the study and how to conduct the use of the schedule. *Honesty and openness* were promoted through an informal daily discussion with the staff, it was thought that this would also increase reliability as the practitioner could check that her observations and findings matched those of others. Hopkins (2002) suggests that colleagues involved in research should have the opportunity to disagree or lodge a protest. Everyone involved had *access to findings*. These were shared with Harry's mum in the interview and all staff from the Centre in a staff meeting. *Researcher effects* have been discussed above and *anonymity* was assured to all of those involved including in writing to Harry's parents.

3.2.4 Sample size and method

[The limits of a small sample size are introduced.]

3.2.5 Validity

To gain validity, research must measure what it aims to measure ... In this study a method of triangulation was used to ensure validity. This involved using contributions from three different points of view, the teacher, the parent and the child.

3.2.6 Reliability

[A comment is made on reliability and the small sample size (Harry). It is accepted that a pilot would have improved reliability.]

3.2.7 Researcher effect

Research performed in the 1920s and 1930s (cited in Roethlisberger and Dickinson 1939) into working conditions found that subjects can perform differently due to the fact that they are part of research, known as the *Hawthorne effect*. As discussed in 3.2.2, observations are part of Foundation Stage practice so research conditions were not too different from normal practice. As an additional measure, the practitioner kept a distance from Harry, just close enough to hear any speech used. The practitioner remained fairly passive during the observations and did not interact with Harry unless he initiated an interaction, apart from to use the schedule with Harry in the second set of observations.

3.2.8 Research schedule

To ensure that the research took place in a methodical and organized fashion and minimized disruption to normal teaching a schedule was followed.

[Research Schedule included.]

3.3 Analysing the research data

The data was analysed using quantitative and qualitative research methods in order to: 'combine the power of words with the authority of numbers' (O'Leary 2004: 18). Throughout the study the observations and interviews were studied and an 'open coding' technique was used to analyse the data as the research took place (Strauss and Corbin 1990), (see Appendix 3). Categories were established to develop the analytic potential of the raw data (Campbell 2004) and were then validated with a search for negative cases. Informal discussions took place with other nursery staff to help the practitioner to gain new information and to seek alternative explanations. Descriptive statistics were calculated for the time Harry spent on tasks with and without a schedule, and also for the number of times Harry got distressed, with and without a schedule.

4.0 Analysis of Findings

[This section discusses the effectiveness of a tailored approach compared to no intervention.]

4.1 The use of a tailored approach

[Both the observations and the interviews showed that a tailored approach was more effective than no intervention. The effectiveness of such an approach at home is described as is the positive effect it has had on Harry's willingness to communicate and the possible negative effect on Harry's socializing with other children. Literature (Kanner 1943; Baron-Cohen 1995; Gabriels 2002; Wedell, 2005 is used in support.]

4.2 Time on task

It was discussed in Section 2.1 that people with autism may lack central coherence (Frith 1989) which may mean that Harry has trouble in concentrating and is easily distracted by environmental stimuli. Prior to the study, Harry could often 'wander' from one activity to another, or show repetitive behaviours (Kanner 1943). Harry had his favourite areas and rarely visited his less favourite activities. The use of a tailored approach helped Harry to spend more time on task and to visit a wider range of areas.

[Harry's time on task is discussed, with statistics and support from literature. Also discussed is the slightly different way in which interventions are used at home (between events) than at nursery (between tasks) (Ozonoff and Cathcart (1998).]

A limitation of this study was that it was difficult to determine when Harry was 'on task'. Often Harry was at an activity but by no means on task. The ambiguity of 'on task' may mean that this study is unreliable and would be difficult to repeat. Perhaps future studies could make a clear definition of what 'on task' would require.

4.3 Reducing the number of times Harry was distressed

[Here the way in which a schedule, both at home and nursery, was important in avoiding Harry becoming distressed or helping to calm him is discussed.]

Harry did not seem to become as distressed as often or as severely during the study as the practitioner had observed on previous occasions, Harry can often be more distressed after the school holidays when returning to nursery. Perhaps a long-term study would truly reflect the effectiveness of the schedule. A criticism of this study may be that it is difficult to define 'distress' and one observer's opinion may differ from another, making this study difficult to repeat. As mentioned above, for observing when Harry was 'on task', perhaps a future study could define this early in the observations.

[The occasions when Harry's Mum found that the schedule was not effective are linked to a discussion of Harry's routine.]

Perhaps routine for Harry is about negatives (such as having to get out of bed or having to have your hair washed) being followed by positives (such as having breakfast at nursery or watching a video), and when an expected positive does not happen, he becomes distressed.

4.4 Other findings

Interestingly, during the first observations Harry was observed teasing other children by hiding objects or running away with them on four occasions. This would suggest that Harry does recognize the mental states of others, contrary to theory of mind (Baron-Cohen 1995). It also supports the ideas that Harry is very much interested in socializing with others, as discussed in Section 4.1.

Prior to the interview, the practitioner was concerned with how Harry's family use the pictures at home. An unexpected finding was that the details of the pictures seemed just as important to Harry's mum as how she used them. Harry's mum talked about some of the symbols being 'too general', and spends a lot of time searching for the pictures they need on the internet.

4.5 Conclusion

The findings are consistent with Dawson and Osterling (1997) who suggest that successful techniques are those which include visual clues, structure and child choice. It seems that a combination of two approaches, TEACCH and PECs met with some success, including increasing time on task and reducing distress. Tutt (2006) warns against combining approaches just because no one intervention has shown that it is highly successful, but most writers agree that there is no 'one size fits all' approach (Hanft and Feinberg 1997; Schreibman 2000; Wall 2004). Harry's mum talked about other interventions she had tried in the past but had not been effective such as Makaton, and suggested that 'trial and error' can be the only way to find out what works, as 'only a parent can know what will work for their child'.

5.0 Conclusions and dissemination

5.1 Aims of the research

The findings were consistent with the literature and showed that the use of a tailored approach was more effective than no intervention (Schreibman 2000). The use of a schedule increased Harry's use of language and also supported Harry at home in making choices at mealtimes. The strategy could be further developed to allow Harry more flexibility to be able to join children spontaneously without having to choose the card first.

The research showed that the use of a schedule helps Harry to stay on task and reduces repetitive behaviour. Although Harry's mum does not use the schedule at home to help Harry to stay on task, she does use it with success to help Harry to move on from one activity to another, as it was useful at nursery.

The use of a schedule did reduce the number of times Harry was distressed at nursery although it was concluded that as Harry was distressed less than normal anyway, a longer research period would be required to truly determine the effectiveness. Harry's mum reported that she relied very much on the schedule at home to avoid distress and to help calm Harry when he was upset. However, she also spoke of times when the intervention did not work.

5.2 Dissemination

Discussions about the use of a schedule for Harry with the staff directly involved have taken place throughout the study and perhaps should have been formally recorded to form a validation group (McNiff 2002). The effectiveness of Harry's schedule have led us to develop a whole class schedule to support all children.

[Further dissemination is discussed.]

5.3 Implications of research

[A method of extending the picture approach to involve all staff is discussed.]
    In Section 4.4, it was suggested that the details of the pictures themselves were just as important in the use of the schedule at home as how the schedule was used. This had not occurred to the practitioner prior to the interview. Informal observations and discussions with another teacher have shown that 'substitute' pictures (for example, using the symbol for play-dough to show a cooking activity) do not work and can be more harmful than using no picture at all. It has been suggested to the special needs coordinator that the nursery could invest in a computer package that provides us with a greater number of pictures or symbols and that one person in nursery could be responsible for printing and laminating them.

5.4 Future research

To ensure progress follows from this action research an action plan has been devised.

[Table 2, Action plan appended.]

5.5 Conclusion

This piece of action research has helped the practitioner and her colleagues to think more critically about their provision. Background research has developed a theoretical understanding of autism which have been shared with other staff to develop an understanding of the needs of children with autism. An effective intervention for Harry has been established and regular discussions with Harry's mum continue to help us to develop our provision.

Appendix 1

Observation.

Appendix 2

Interview Questions.

Appendix 3

Categories Found.

Observations

On task	(no communication)
On task	Cs) Communication to self/noises
	C) Communicating with others
	Ci) Initiating communication with others
	C2) Communicating with others by teasing

Not on task, wandering
WCs) Talking to self

Communicating	C1) Interaction during activity that is not play, e.g. dinnertime
	C1i) Initiating communication during non-play activities

Distressed	a) Not prepared for change
	b) Another child's actions
	c) Frustration, cannot complete a task

Following instructions, following routine
FCs) Talking to self

Not understanding, not following instructions (but not distressed)

Refusal to follow routine, refusal to comply

Attempts made by adult to alter routine to Harry's expectations

Unproductive behaviour (hitting, throwing, lying on floor)

a) Appears unhappy
b) Appears excited

Choosing from pictures/being shown routine using pictures

Approaching adult because wants to choose picture

Interview

Positive remarks about use of schedule

When and how the family use it

How she came to use it, who

Details about the pictures themselves

Other interventions and strategies

- pointing
- Makaton
- drawing

Explanations

Thoughts

Examples

What happens when don't use

When it doesn't work/don't use

- ambiguous pictures
- understands but not happy about changes
- necessary to rpt whole routine
- clothes

References

Audit Commission (2002) *Special Educational Needs: A Mainstream Issue.* London: Audit Commission.

Baron-Cohen, S. (1995) *Mindblindness: An Essay on Autism and Theory of Mind.* London: Bradford Books.

British Educational Research Association (BERA) (2003) *Ethical Guidelines for Educational Research*.

Bondy, A.S. and Frost, L. (2002) *A Picture's Worth: PECS and Other Visual Communication Strategies in Autism*. Bethesda: Woodbine House.

Brown, A. and Dowling, P. (1998) *Doing Research/Reading Research: A Mode of Interrogation for Education*. London: The Falmer Press.

Burton, D. and Bartlett, S. (2005) *Practitioner Research for Teachers*. London: Paul Chapman Publishing.

Campbell, A. (2004) *Practitioner Research and Professional Development in Education*. London: Paul Chapman Publishing.

Clough, P. and Nutbrown, C. (2002) The index for inclusion: personal perspectives from early years educators. *Early Education*, 36(Spring): 1–4.

Convery, C. (1998) A teacher's response to 'reflection-in-action', *Cambridge Journal of Education*, 28(2): 197–205.

Danziger, K. (1990) *Constructing the Subject: Historical Origins of Psychological Research*. Cambridge: Cambridge University Press.

Dawson, G. and Osterling, A. (1997) Early intervention in autism, in M.J. Guralnick (ed.) *The Effectiveness of Early Intervention*. Baltimore, MD: Paul H. Brookes.

Denscombe, M. (1998) *The Good Research Guide*. Buckingham: Open University Press.

Department for Education and Science (DES) (1978) *Special Educational Needs: Report of the Committee of Enquiry into the Education of Handicapped Children and Young People (The Warnock Report)*. London: Her Majesty's Stationery Office.

Department for Education and Skills/Department of Health DfES/DoH (2002) *Autistic Spectrum Disorders: Good Practice Guidance*. Nottingham: DfES.

Department for Education and Skills (DfES) (2004) *Removing Barriers to Achievement: The Government's Strategy for SEN*. London: DfES.

Dowling, P.C. (1998) *The Sociology of Mathematics Education: Mathematical Myths/Pedagogic Texts*. London: Falmer Press.

Elliott, J. (1991) *Action Research for Educational Change*. Buckingham: Open University Press.

Frith, U. (1989) *Autism: Explaining the Enigma*. Oxford: Blackwell.

Gabriels, R.L. (2002) *Autism: From Research to Individualized Practice*. London: Jessica Kingsley Publishers.

Glasser, B.G. and Strauss, A. (1967) Discovery of grounded theory: strategies for qualitative research. *Sociology Press*, 1.

Green, V., Pituch, K.A., Itchon, J., Choi, A., O'Reilly, M. and Sigafoos, J. (2006) Internet survey of treatments used by parents of children with autism, *Research in Developmental Disabilities*, 27(1): 70–84.

Hanbury, M. (2005) *Educating Pupils with Autistic Spectrum Disorders: A Practical Guide*. London: Paul Chapman Publishing.

Hanft, B.E. and Feinberg, E. (1997) Toward the development of a framework for determining the frequency and intensity of early intervention services, *In Young Children* 10(1): 27–37.

Hewitt, S. (2005) *Specialist Support Approaches to Autism Spectrum Disorder Students in Mainstream Settings*. London: Jessica Kingsley Publishers.

Hopkins, D. (1998) *A Teacher's Guide to Classroom Research*. Maidenhead: Open University Press.

Hopkins, D. (2002) *A Teacher's Guide to Classroom Research*, 3rd edn. Maidenhead: Open University Press.

Howlin, P. (2005) *Assessing the Effectiveness of Early Intervention Programmes for Young Children with Autism*. Available at: http://www.nas.org.uk/nas/jsp/polopoly.jsp?d=693&a=7972. [accessed 4 January 2007].

Kanner, L. (1949) Problems of nosology and psychodynamics of early infantile autism, *American Journal of Orthopsychiatry*, 19: 416–26.

Koshy, V. (2005) *Action Research for Improving Practice*. London: Paul Chapman Publishing.

Lewin, K. (1948) *Resolving Social Conflicts: Selected Papers on Group Dynamics*. New York: Harper & Row.

Lord, C. (1995) Follow-up of two year olds referred for possible autism, *Journal of Child Psychology and Psychiatry*, 36: 1365–82.

Maine (2000) cited in Howlin, P. (2005) *Assessing the Effectiveness of Early Intervention Programmes for Young Children with Autism*. Available at: http://www.nas.org.uk/nas/jsp/polopoly.jsp?d=693&a=7972 [accessed 4 January 2007].

Maslow, A. (1943) A theory of human motivation. *Psychological Review*, 50: 370–96.

DOING CLASSROOM RESEARCH

A Step-by-Step Guide for Student Teachers

Sally Elton-Chalcraft, Alice Hansen and Samantha Twiselton

- Are you worried about doing your classroom-based research project?
- Do you feel daunted at the prospect of carrying out a literature review?
- Does the thought of collecting and analyzing data make you panic?

If you answer 'yes' to any of these questions, then this is the book for you!

Written in an informal style, this is the essential, practical and accessible step-by-step guide for all teacher-training students, who in addition to facing the enormous challenge of training to become a teacher, also have to conduct their own classroom-based research.

It contains three sections that mirror the process of doing classroom research. From getting started and choosing appropriate research strategies, to making your findings public, the book covers the whole range of issues to help you succeed with what can seem like a daunting task.

Each of the chapters offers gentle guidance and support at every stage of the research process. Topics covered include:

- The purpose of school-based research
- Guidance on how to carry out a literature review
- Research ethics
- The impacts of research on children's and students' learning
- Methods of data collection and analysis
- Ways of sharing research with a wider audience
- Opportunities for continued professional development

Doing Classroom Research is a must for every teacher-training student.

Contents: *List of figures and tables – Contributors – Foreword – Part I Introduction – What's in it for me? – Moving from reflective practitioner to practitioner researcher – Part II Getting started – Survival skills – Information skills for classroom research – Ethical issues – Reliability and validity – Part III Research strategies – Doing research in the classroom – Intervention, innovation and creativity in the classroom: Using findings to improve practice – Collaborative research – Analysis of data – Part IV Writing it up and making it public – Presenting research in writing – Presenting research in a range of forums – Next steps – Index.*

2008   184pp

978-0-335-22876-8 (Paperback)   978-0-335-22875-1 (Hardback)

APPROACHES TO LEARNING

A Guide for Teachers

Anne Jordan, Orison Carlile and Annetta Stack

'This book provides a really sound grounding in the theories that underpin successful teaching and learning. Without over-simplification it provides accessible introductions to the key learning theories with which teachers and students are likely to engage, and it has immense practical value.'

Professor Sally Brown, Pro-Vice-Chancellor,
Leeds Metropolitan University, UK

This comprehensive guide for education students and practitioners provides an overview of the major theories of learning. It considers their implications for policy and practice and sets out practical guidelines for best pedagogical practice.

The book can be read as a series of stand-alone chapters or as an integrated overview of theoretical perspectives drawn from the philosophy, psychology, sociology and pedagogy that guide educational principles and practice. Each chapter contains:

- An accessible introduction to each theory
- A summary of key principles
- Critical insights drawn from the theories discussed
- Examples and illustrations from contemporary research and practice
- Summary boxes that highlight critical and key points made
- Practical implications for education professionals

Approaches to Learning is an invaluable resource for students and practitioners who wish to reflect on their educational constructs and explore and engage in the modern discourse of education.

Contents: *List of figures and tables – Acknowledgements – Introduction – Philosophy of education – Behaviourism – Cognitivism – Constructivism – Social learning – Cultural learning – Intelligence – Life course development – Adult learning – Values – Motivation – The learning body – Language and learning – Experiential and competency-based learning – Inclusivity – Blended learning – The future – Glossary.*

2008   304pp

978-0-335-22670-2 (Paperback)   978-0-335-22671-9 (Hardback)

DEVELOPING THINKING; DEVELOPING LEARNING

A Guide to Thinking Skills in Education

Debra McGregor

'This highly informative book provides a comprehensive guide to the teaching of thinking skills in primary and secondary education.'

Learning and Teaching Update

It is now recognised that thinking skills, such as problem-solving, analysis, synthesis, creativity and evaluation, can be nurtured and developed, and education professionals can play a significant role in shaping the way that children learn and think. As a result, schools are being encouraged to make greater use of thinking skills in lessons and the general emphasis on cognition has developed considerably. This book offers a comprehensive introduction to thinking skills in education and provides detailed guidance on how teachers can support cognitive development in their classrooms.

Developing Thinking; Developing Learning discusses how thinking programmes, learning activities and teachers' pedagogy in the classroom can fundamentally affect the nature of pupils' thinking, and considers the effects of the learning environment created by peers and teachers. It compares the nature, design and outcomes of established thinking programmes used in schools and also offers practical advice for teachers wishing to develop different kinds of thinking capabilities.

This is an indispensable guide to thinking skills in schools today, and is key reading for education studies students, teachers and trainee teachers, and educational psychologists.

Contents: List of figures and tables – Acknowledgements – Introduction – What do we mean by 'thinking?' – What kind of thinking should we encourage children to do? – Thinking and learning – The nature of thinking programmes developed within a subject context – The nature of general thinking skills programmes – The nature of infusing thinking – Effectiveness of thinking programmes – Development of creative thinking – Development of critical thinking – Development of metacognition – Development of problem solving capability – Synthesising the general from the particular – Professional development to support thinking classrooms – School development to support thinking communities – References – Index.

2007   344pp

978-0-335-21780-9 (Paperback)   978-0-335-21781-6 (Hardback)

USING SECONDARY DATA IN EDUCATIONAL AND SOCIAL RESEARCH

Emma Smith

Secondary data is a powerful tool for providing context to an otherwise small-scale study, as well as being an efficient way of bringing together a large amount of data, particularly where access to the field may be difficult.

This comprehensive guide introduces students to the use of secondary data in educational and social research, and provides a practical resource for researchers who are new to the field of secondary data analysis. The author encourages researchers to consider the potential for using secondary data both as their primary research method, but also as a useful strategy in mixed methods designs.

The first part of the book explores the role of secondary data analysis in contemporary social research. It considers the arguments for and against its use and addresses its particular benefits in mixed method research designs, especially those in the political arithmetic tradition.

The second part introduces worked examples which show the potential for using secondary sources to answer a varied range of research questions. It provides step-by-step guidance on how to manipulate and analyse secondary data. The inclusion of recent national and international datasets as exemplars allows students to place their research in a 'real life' context and to consider current and topical research issues.

2008   210pp

978-0-335-22358-9 (Paperback)   978-0-335-22357-2 (Hardback)